Jessica Angel
As Above, So Below

Curated by Holly Crawford

December 12, 2013 – February 22, 2014

Copyright © 2013 AC Institute
All Rights Reserved
Published by the AC Institute
547 W. 27th Street, Suite 210
New York, NY 10001
www.artcurrents.org

ISBN: 978-1939901033

AC Institute

Since its inception in 2004, the AC Institute's mission has been to advance the understanding of the arts through investigation, research and education. It is a lab and forum for experimentation and critical discussion. We support and develop projects that explore a performative exchange across visual, sonic, verbal and experiential disciplines. We encourage critical writing that challenges conventional expectations of meaning and objectivity as well as the boundaries between the rational and subjective.

The AC Institute is a nonprofit 501(c)(3) organization under the direction of Holly Crawford.

Table of Contents

Preface   i
by Holly Crawford

Micro Cosmic   ii
by Nicole Bebout

As Above So Below   1
by Jessica Angel

Maquette   11

Table of Contents

Hemispherical Immersions	17
Enter the Wall	23
The Self of the Building	29
Building Codes	33
Info-Trek	37
Inside the Computing Machine	41
About Jessica Angel	47

Preface

Jessica Angel's installation AS ABOVE, SO BELOW takes over the South Gallery of the AC Institute. Angel transforms the gallery into an enormous microchip that mirrors the enormity of the cosmos. Using black vinyl cut-outs of angular shapes placed on the white walls, Angel creates a complex perspectival system that suggests the warping of space and time.

I want to thank Jessica Angel and everyone who works at AC Institute, Eliana Blechman, Eddy Villatoro, Nicole Bebout and James Dillenbeck, for their work on this exhibition.

Holly Crawford, Ph.D.
Director

Micro Cosmic
by Nicole Bebout

Jessica Angel creates site-specific immersive installations that expand a location's boundaries by collapsing them. At the AC Institute, Angel's AS ABOVE, SO BELOW erases the walls through a painted mirage of black and white forms read as a magnified and distorted microchip. The shapes swirl and pull toward the corners of the gallery, visually disorienting the viewer and transporting them into an immense universe that simultaneously fits snuggly within a 500 square foot gallery space. Angel's process of merging the 'large' with the 'small' mirrors the streams of virtual data through microchips, Angel's preferred symbol of our contemporary virtual society. Angel is interested in representing the human within the cosmic movement of virtual data. For her 2013 installation, Hemispherical Immersions, Angel asks: How can we make a visual immersion into cyberspace? What kind of imagery can evoke this ethereal space filled up with information? Would this be a paradise-like space full of light and color? Or, would this place be instead polluted and excessive just as some parts of our real planet are?

In Hemispherical Immersions, cyberspace is represented as a visual warbling distortion of black and white blocks against a vibrantly pixilated environment. The installation was made in conjunction with a series of mixed media paintings Angel also created in 2013, Panoptics and Panoramas. The emphasis on geometric structures and spaces symbolized the "new geography" of a virtual globalized world created from the free flow of information. Her paintings, as the title suggests, are a theoretical counterpoint to the more buoyant installation, ominously hinting at a virtual world that is as congested, crowded and territorial as the physical one.

AS ABOVE, SO BELOW more fully realizes Angel's visualization of information "as a dynamic force." Through her painted vortex, Angel harkens back to the dynamism of the Futurists. This turn of the century group of avant-garde painters celebrated the technological and mechanical advances being made around them through the formal investigation of motion and speed as the best representation of their time. As a formal artistic investigation, Angel replaces the physical motion and speed of the Futurists with virtual data that flows through cyber networks.

Angel's paintings and installations represent the structure of atoms, computer chips, city blocks and the cosmos, all at the same time. The human body in all of this seems at odds with the virtual, at once like a large lump of ungainly flesh and hopelessly puny and obsolete. Her complex perspectives playfully visualize the infinite dimensions of the virtual and propel the viewer into their near-future virtual existence.

Angel subscribes to the philosophy that the next step in human evolution is virtual. As the researcher Charlie Mansfield explains, "The virtual is not the false nor the imaginary. The virtual is the power that something has of becoming something. A tree is virtually present in a seed." We march toward the virtual future. In the absence of the physical there is the promise of the infinite, a unity of experience and the potential for peace and joy; one hopes for the paradise that Angel mused into being.

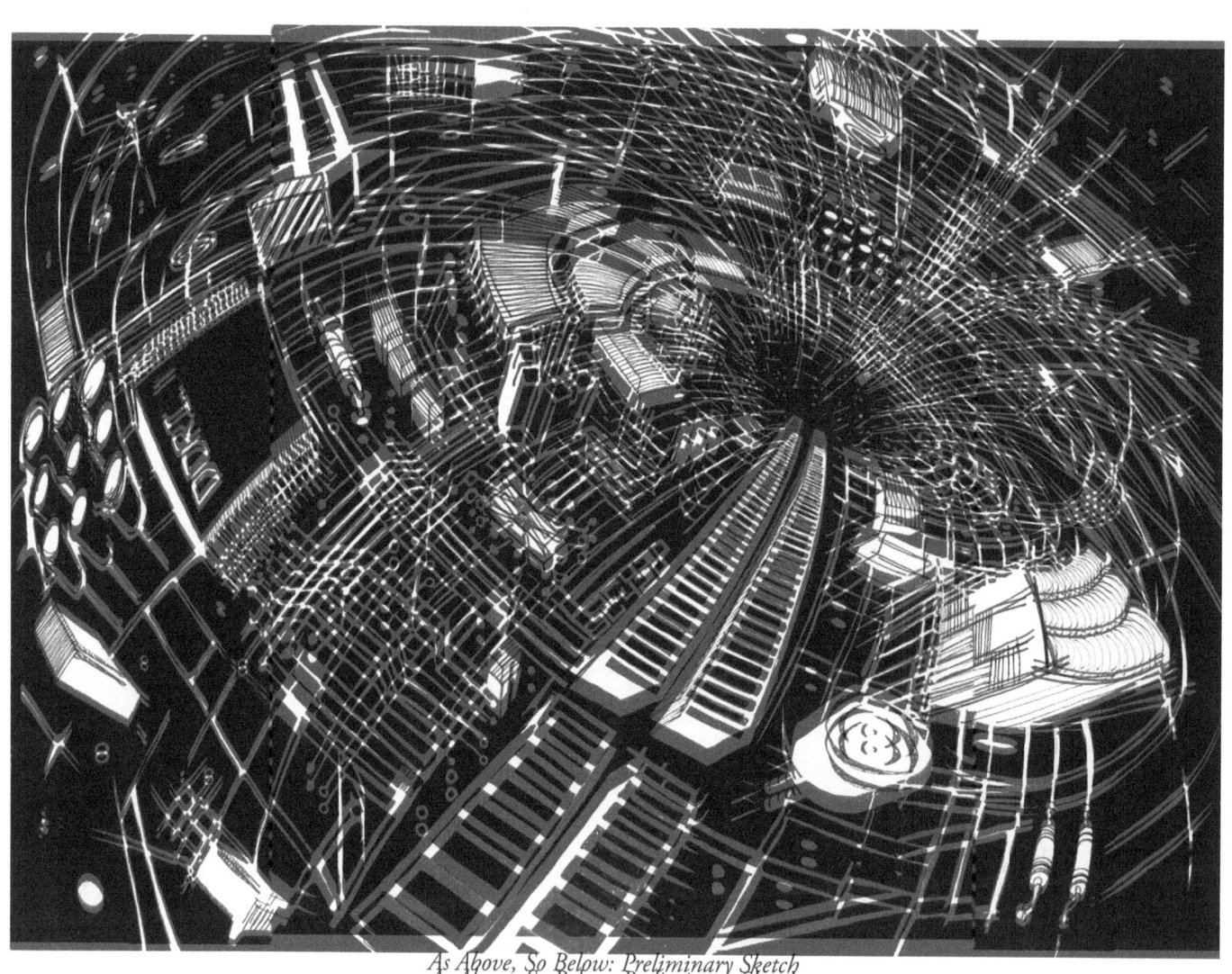

As Above, So Below: Preliminary Sketch

As Above, So Below

AC Institute
New York, NY

December 12, 2013 – February 22, 2014
Curated by Holly Crawford

As Above, So Below - New York, NY

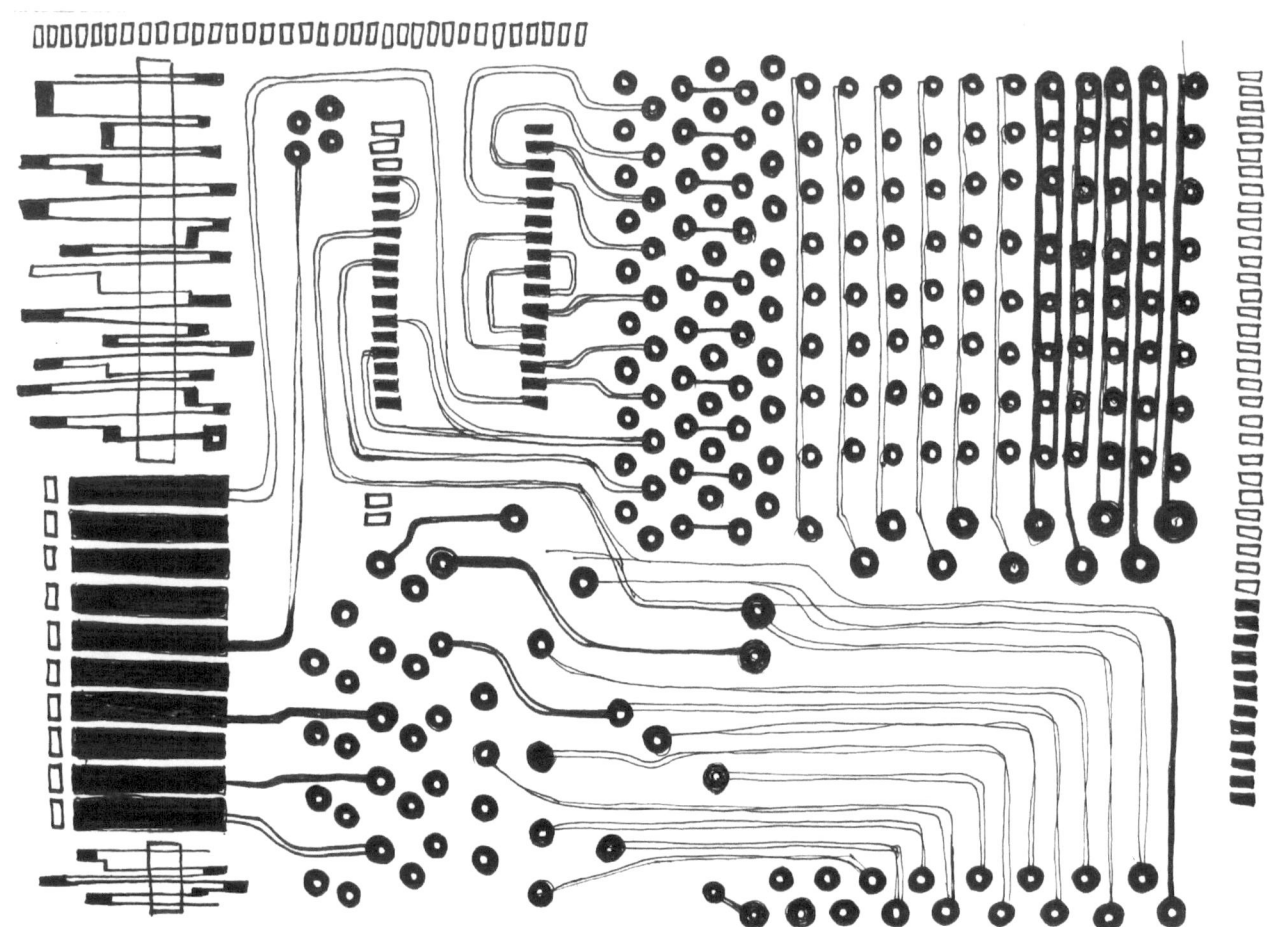

Integratded Circuits, 10" x 7" China Ink on Paper
Preliminary Sketch for As Above, So Below

As Above, So Below - New York, NY

"The 'Strange Loop' phenomenon occurs whenever, by moving upwards (or downwards) through levels of some hierarchical system, we unexpectedly find ourselves right back where we started."
Douglas Hofstadter

"That which is Below corresponds to that which is Above, and that which is Above corresponds to that which is Below, to accomplish the miracle of the One Thing." Thus, whatever happens on any level of reality (physical, emotional, or mental) also happens on every other level.
"The Emerald Tablet of Hermes Trismegistus"

As Above, So Below - New York, NY

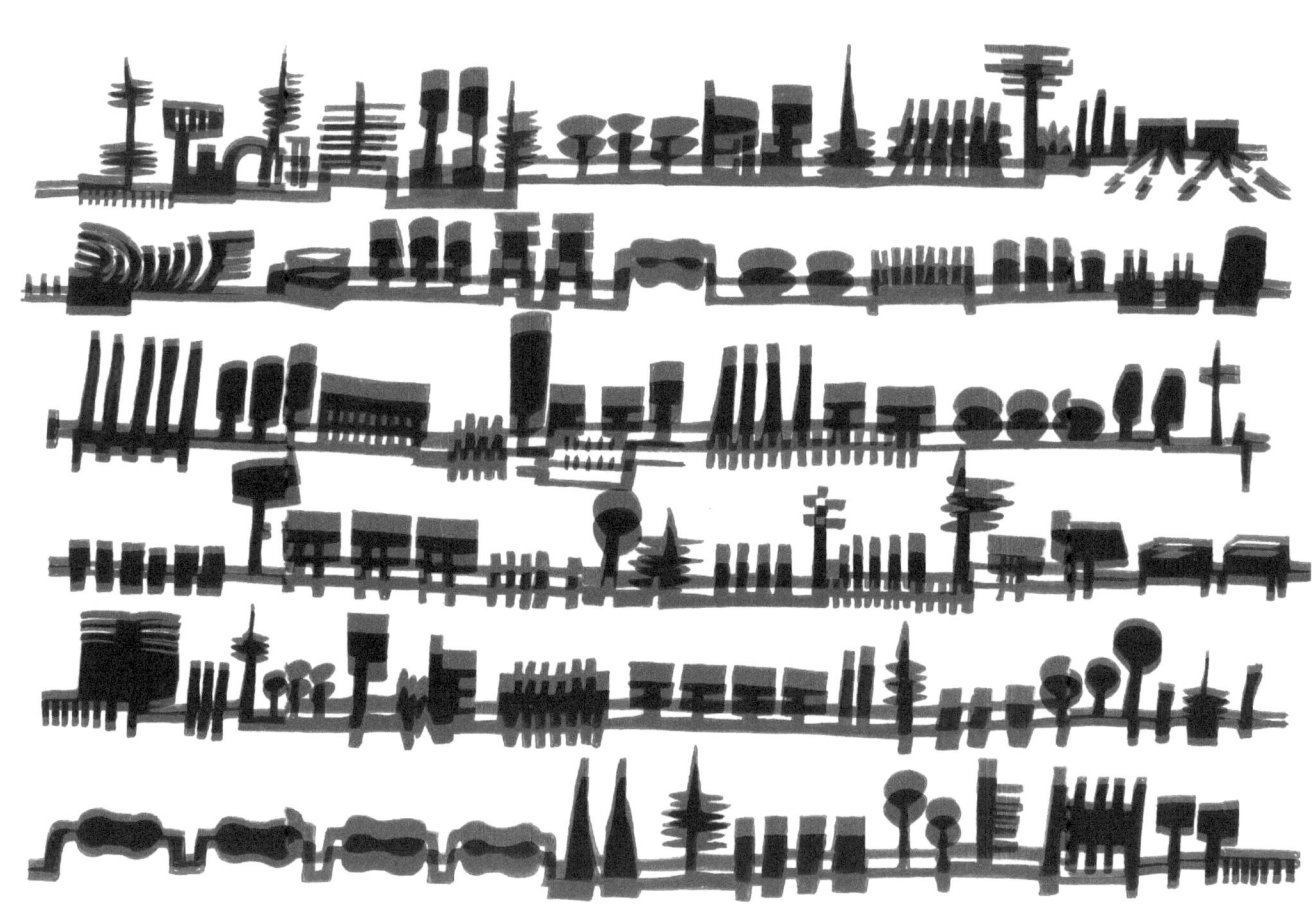

Circuit City, 10" x 7", China Ink on Paper
Preliminary Sketch for As Above, So Below

As Above, So Below - New York, NY

INTRODUCTION

The solar system can easily be paralleled with the "basic" unit of matter, the atom. Operations of a colossal city are analogous to the miniature calculations of a computer. Phenomena of any system occur every instant, simultaneously, on small and large scales. I am interested in exploring these patterns and parallel realities, this duality between the vast and the minute. The deeper into the minute one goes, the closer one gets to understanding the large and vice versa.

I have chosen two specific analogies to embody the idea of the minute and the vast as equivalents 1) the relationship between the outer space and the digital information space and 2) the similarity between urban planning and computer integrated circuits.

To work around this dichotomy I will create an immersive installation that takes over the northern room of the AC Institute. I plan to "invert" these two ideas representing the "large" in a small scale and the "minute" in an outsized scale, emphasizing the concept of the strange loop and the cyclic patterns. The installation will make reference to the micro world of computers in correlation with outer space phenomena.

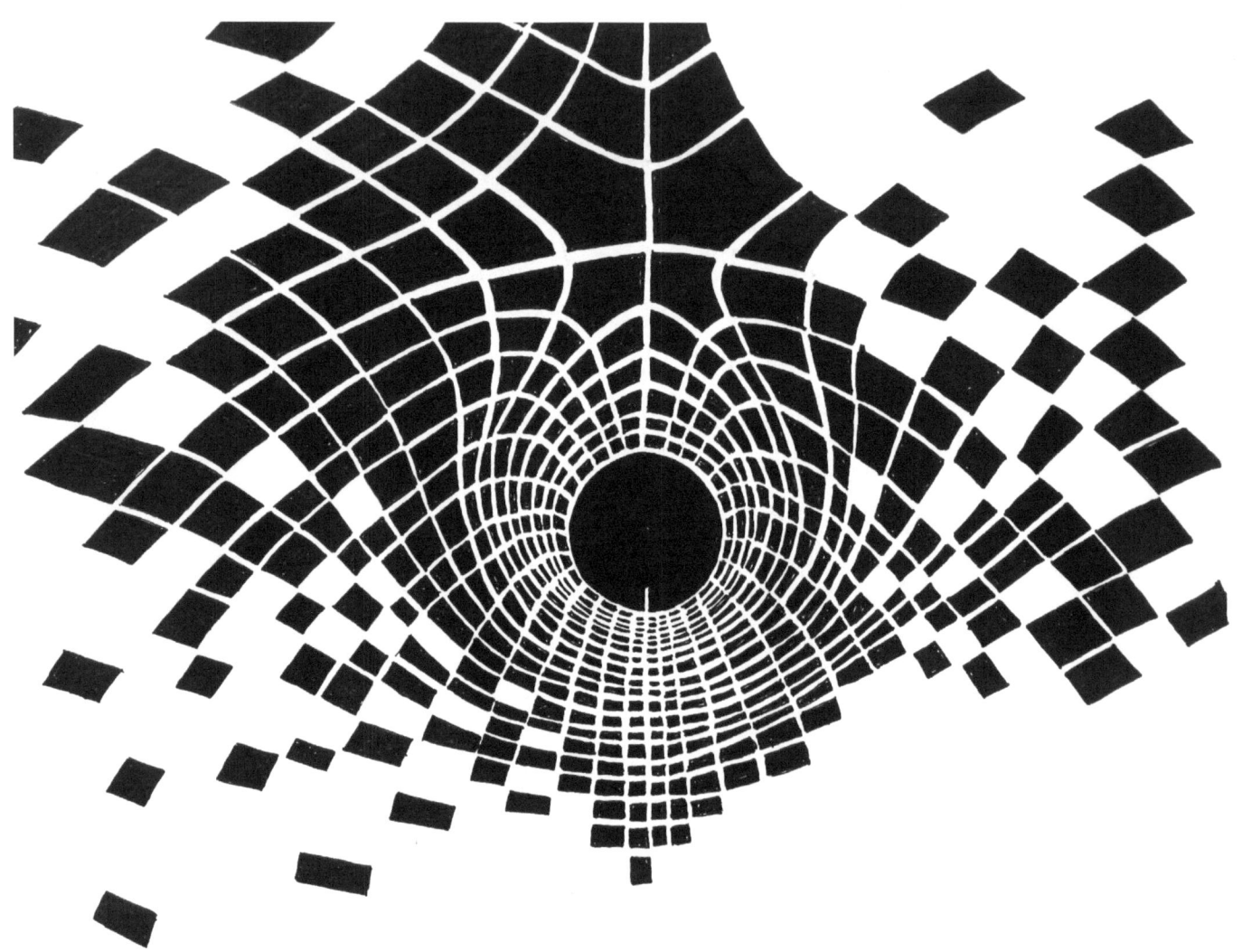

Untitled, 10" x 7" China Ink on Paper
Preliminary Sketch for As Above, So Below

CONCEPTUAL BASIS

The Vast Space of Surrounding Information

    The more we connect to the net of human understanding recorded in books and the internet, the more we realize there are immense amounts of data that we will never be able to grasp. Human knowledge is an ancient "living" being that crosses throughout history because the mesh of information is as old as writing itself. The branched pattern of this net is similar to that of a system, in which you plug-into and start traveling through, finding yourself in an endless universe. I can't help comparing this virtual space where information flows, to the outer space; Clusters of ideas bundled together, sharing a common essence, rotate around a central theme, while other groups of ideas rotate around the opposite theme complementarily. The two groups of ideas appear to work in a corresponding way, where negative and positive, true and false, cannot be one without the other. (Dionysius could not exist if it wasn't for Apollo or vice versa) Numerous questions rise when I address these similes. Where is this ethereal place where ideas flow located? Can we relate the behavior of information to atomic or cosmological behaviors?

As Above, So Below - New York, NY

Erasing the Limits of Space

Speed, war, love, theft, commerce, crowds – everything we know to be characteristic of a contemporary city, has been codified. A mirrored virtual image of the "outside" has been created inside our computing machines. The ways our cities are planned seem to correlate to the structure of a motherboard. Even if we go further into the microscope we find the structures of neurons to be remarkably similar to that of cities. Are these resemblances related to the nature of interconnectivity? Why are these natural and artificial forms so similar and is there such a difference between the two? Can we compare the micro-structure of computer integrated circuits to the mega-structure of the universe?

DESCRIPTION AND PROCESS

Using black adhesive vinyl over the walls, floor and ceiling of the room, I will depict an outer-space scene inspired in images of microchips. I will "enlarge" the micro world of computer electronics and "reduce" the macro-cosmos to the size of the gallery space. The installation will seem like a black hole in the corner of the room that sucks in the space-time mesh where urban looking, three-dimensional objects will be placed. Using complex perspective techniques, this spatially transformative mural will create the effect that the gallery boundaries have been erased.

As Above, So Below - New York, NY

PUBLIC PROGRAMING

This project aims to foster cross-disciplinary initiatives enabling forms of collaboration among sciences, philosophy, music, art and new media, in order to create a collective environment crucial for contemporary practices. Five different sessions will take place inside the installation space, where guests will host lectures, performances and interventions around the ideas addressed by Jessica Angel.

Thursday December 19th 2013, 6 - 8 pm
Live Footage *Music Performance*

Live Footage is often described as some of the finest "surrealist soundtrack composers" in the making by scoring some of the most eclectic contemporary pieces in film, fashion, dance and in tune composing their own music.

Thursday January 16th 2014, 6 - 8 pm
Three-Dimensional and Interactive / *Nelson Ramon*

In collaboration with Jessica Angel, Nelson will build three-dimensional elements and incorporate technological components in order to increase the immersive experience of the installation. Sensors will trigger visual and audio narratives that will invite the audience to modify, alter and interact with the space and they way they perceive it.

Thursday January 30th 2014, 7 - 8 pm
Does Infinity Have a Size? / *Jaclyn Avidon*

Jaclyn will discuss what the concept of infinity means in mathematics, and how we can show that there are multiple types of infinity. As long as you know how to count, you can see that just as infinity has many representations in art, it also has many representations in mathematics.

Thursday February 13th 2014, 6-8 pm
Performance Intervention / *Soler*

Soler will do a performance based, intervention work, responding to the place and time of the show as well as taking into account the people in its surroundings. Soler describes Jessica's installation "as a space of sculptural extrusion", where he will be making actions tangible in a visceral manner responding to this given condition.

Thursday February 20th 2014, 6–8 pm
Sounds Above / Vibrates Below / *Gilberto Castillo*

"Sounds Above/Vibrates Below" is a work based on a simple melody, which is deconstructed to slowly distribute its subtracted elements in simultaneous pitch and rhythmic planes, generating a rather spaced static texture. Another layer interacts with the melodic texture, shifting between synthetic sounds and field recordings of natural elements, human chants, city rumbles, and other soundscapes, aiming to reflect the similarities of one into each other. This piece has been created under the same concepts and ideas as the exhibition "As above, so below" from Jessica Angel.

As Above, So Below - New York, NY

Maquette
As Above, So Below

As Above, So Below - Maquette

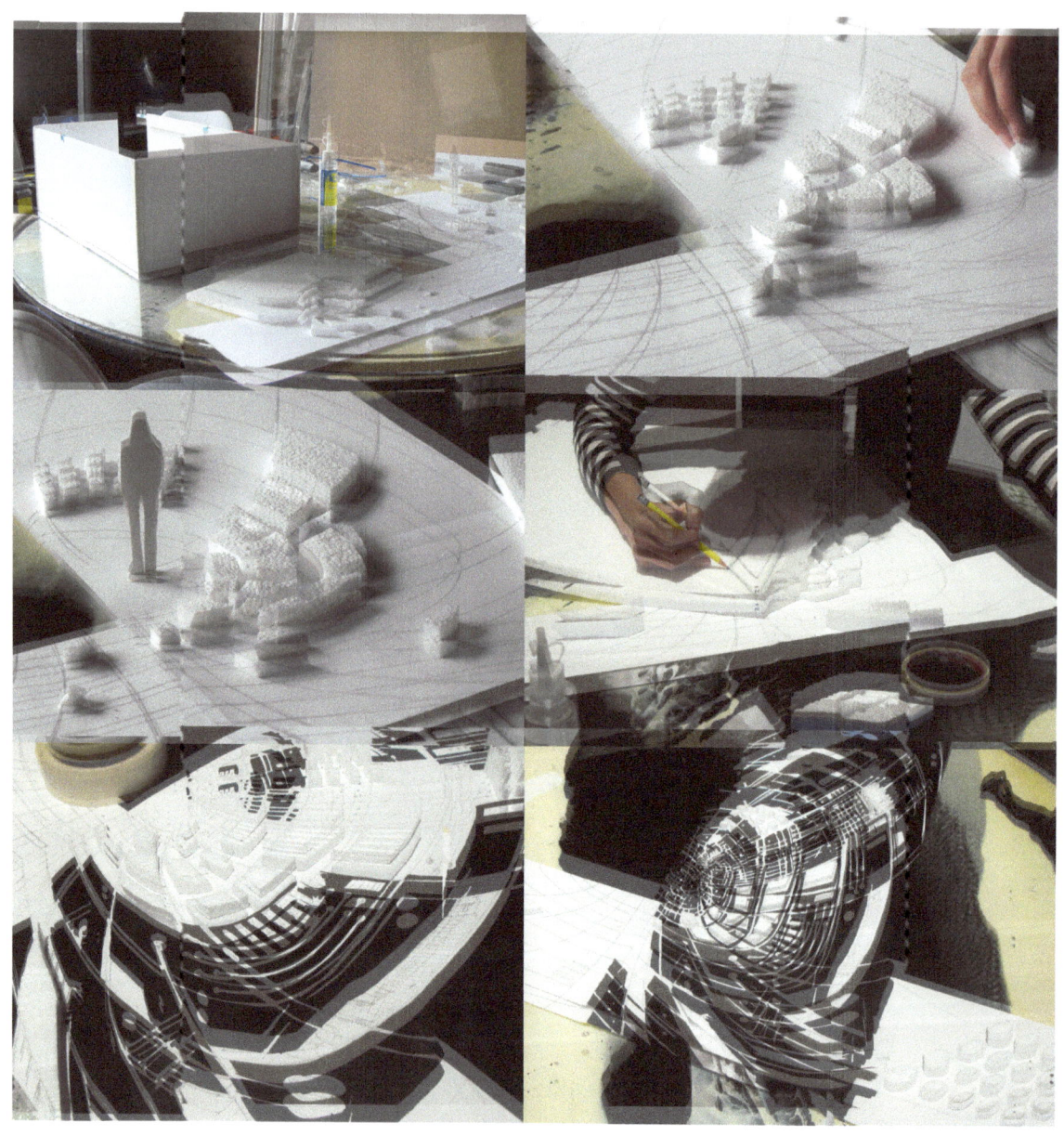

As Above, So Below - Maquette

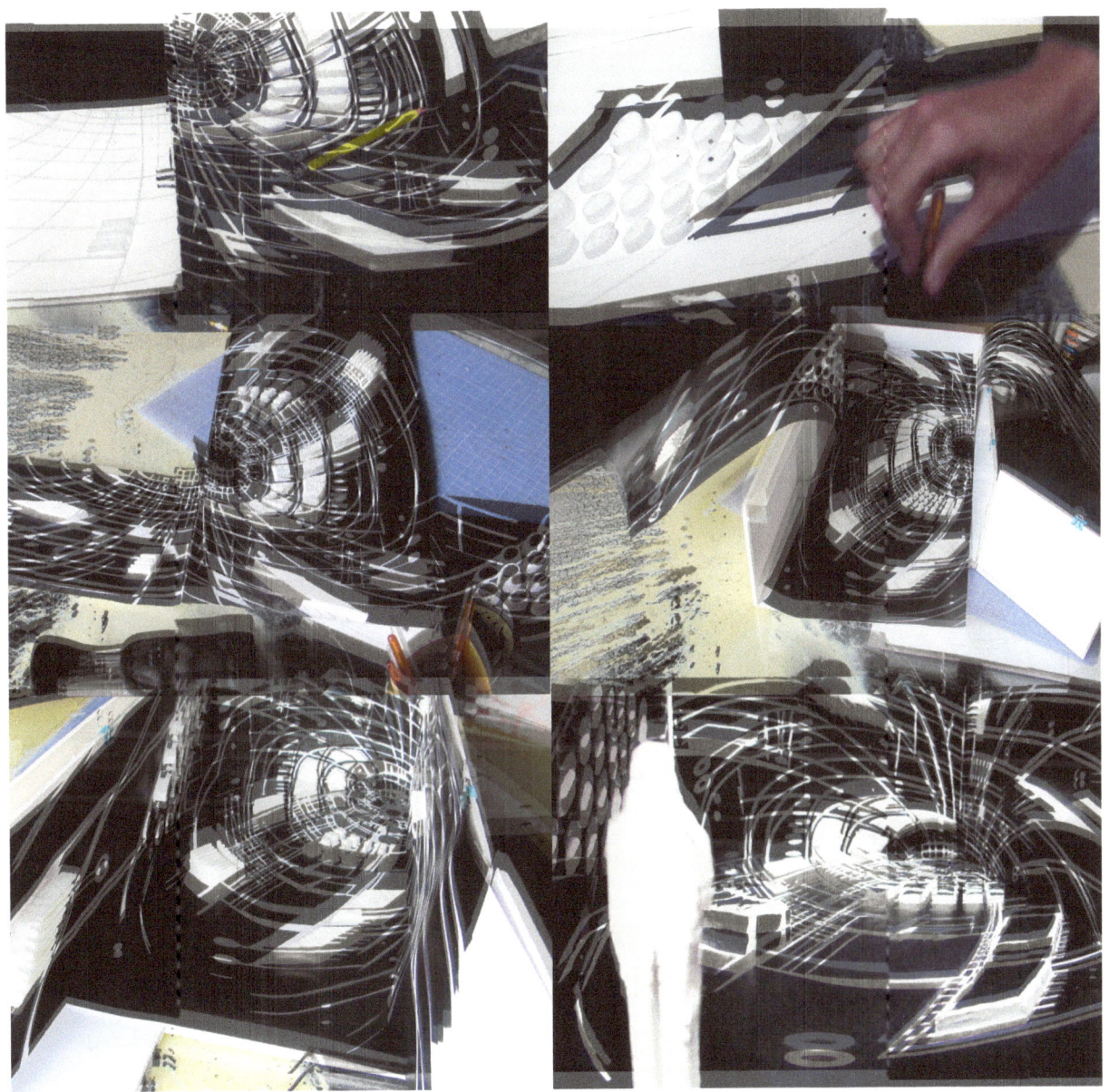

As Above, So Below: Maquette Video Stills 1 and 2

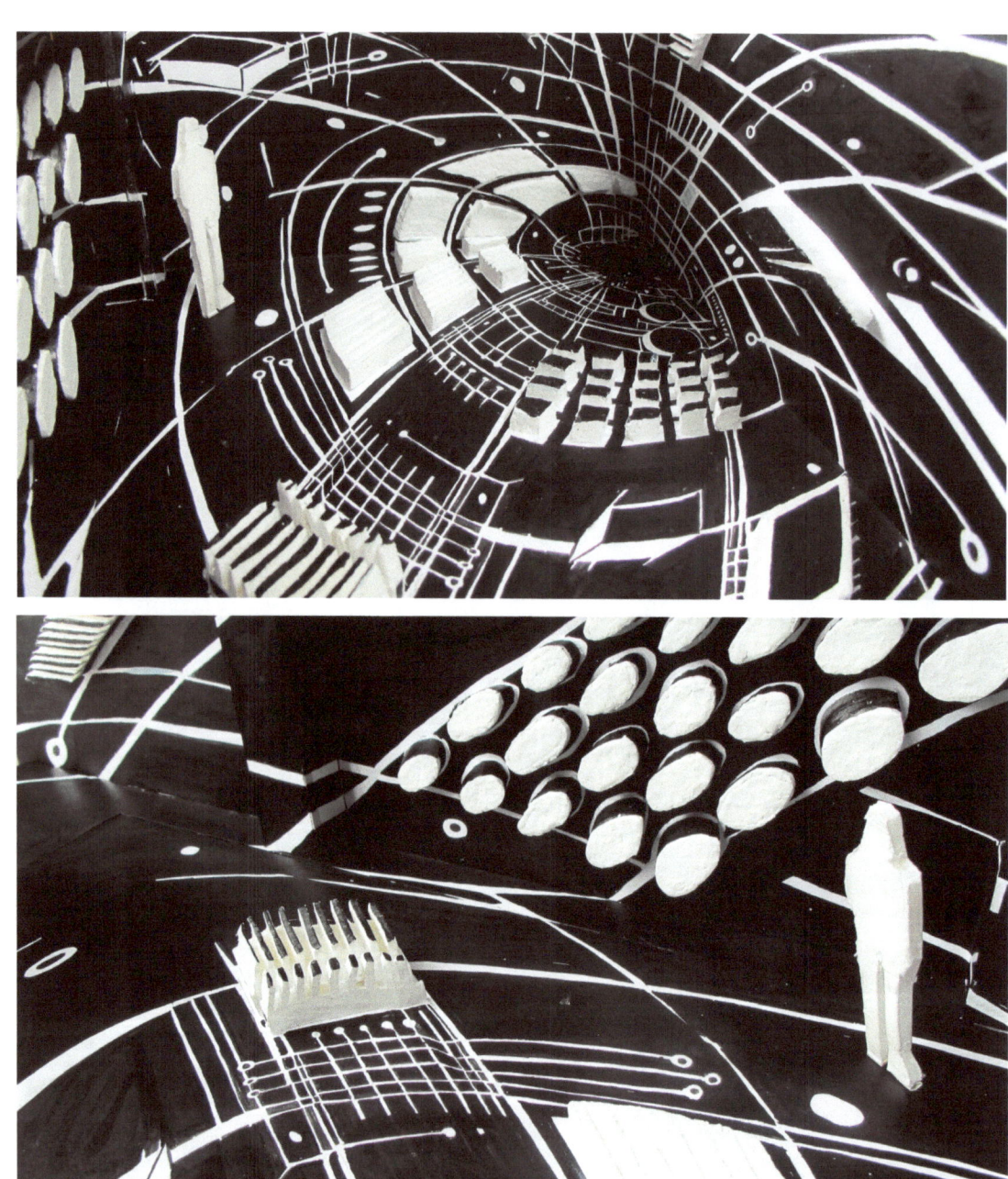

As Above, So Below: Maquette 1 and 2

As Above, So Below - Maquette

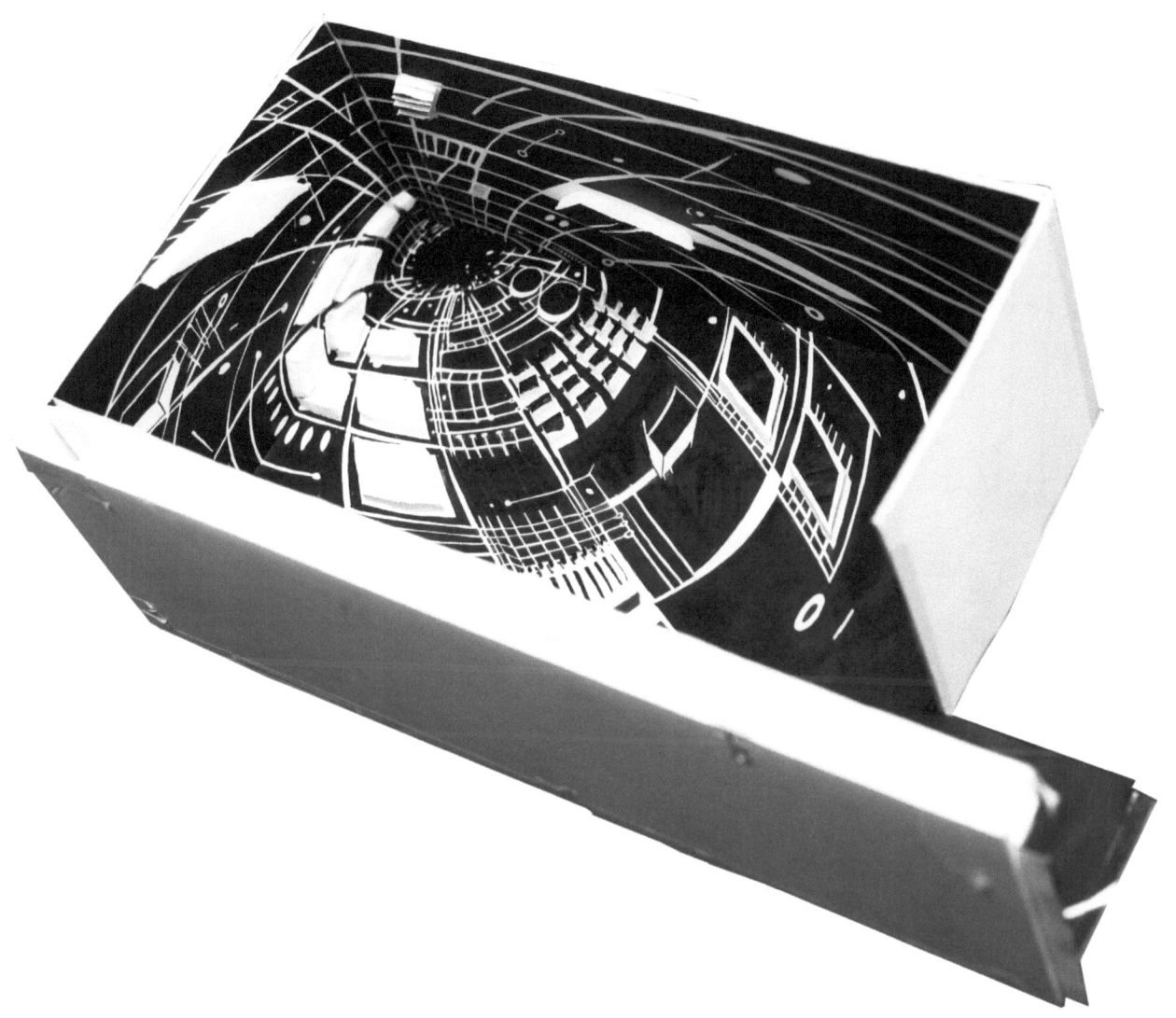

As Above, So Below: Maquette 12" X 22" X 7" China ink on paper, Foamboard.

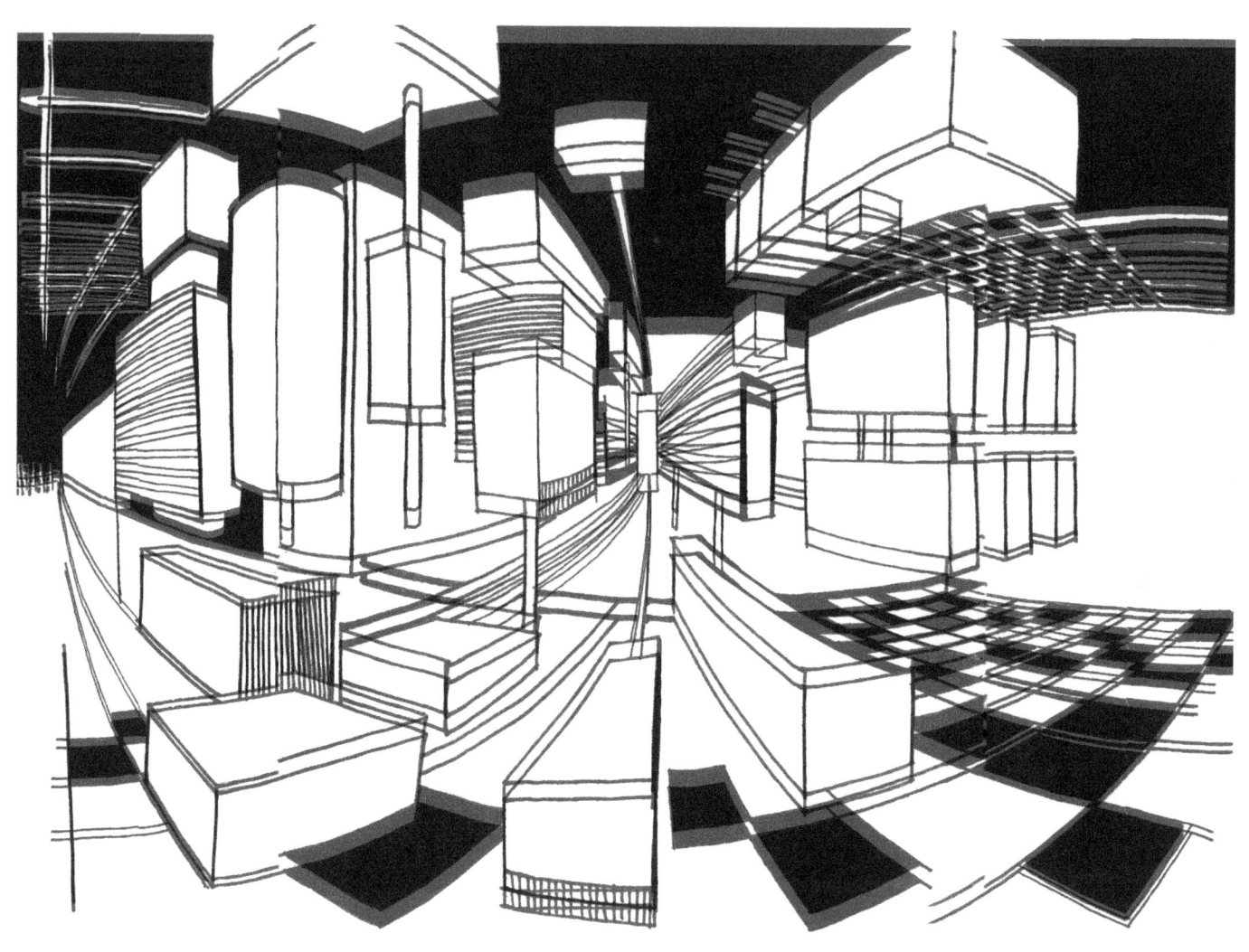

Panoramic, 10" x 7" China Ink on Paper
Preliminary Sketch for Hemispherical Immersion

Hemispherical Immersion
Bogotá, Colombia 2013

Hemispherical Immersion - Bogotá, Colombia - 2013

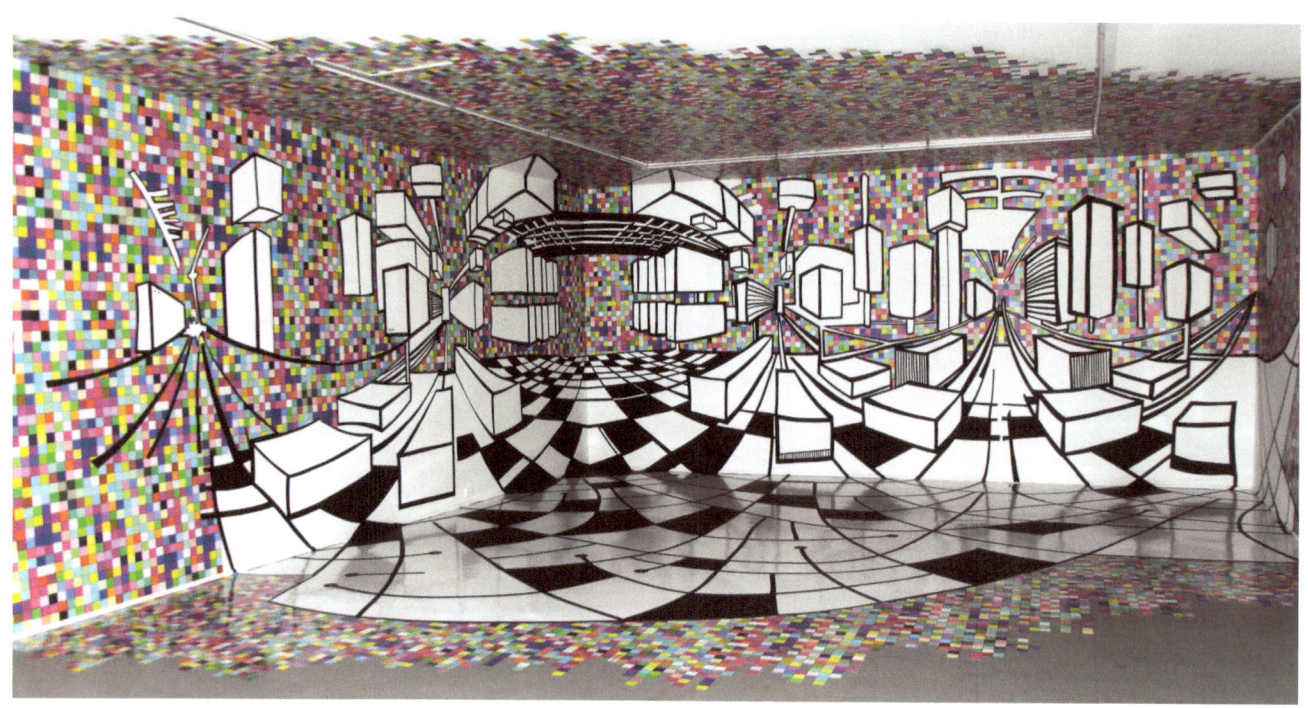

Hemispherical Immersion: Image 1

Hemispherical Immersion - Bogotá, Colombia - 2013

How can we make a visual immersion into cyberspace? What kind of imagery can evoke this ethereal space filled up with information? Would this be a paradise-like space full of light and color? Or, would this place be instead polluted and excessive just as some parts of our real planet are?

Based on the concepts described by Paul Virilio and Pierre Lévy I produced in the main room of Juan Salas Gallery in Bogotá, an immersive installation with adhesive vinyl and off-set prints pasted on walls ceiling and floor. This installation fuses with the exhibition space where pieces of the series Panoptics and Panoramas are located. Gilberto Castillo's sound design is an important part of this piece.

I am interested here in playing with the paradox between traditional media and the digital image in order to expose an analogy between the real and the virtual. I am inclined to working with

Cómo podemos hacer una inmersión visual dentro del ciberespacio? Que tipo de imaginario puede evocar este no-lugar etéreo cargado de información? Sería éste un espacio paradisíaco lleno de luz y color? O sería por el contrario un lugar polucionado acorde a los excesos que tenemos sobre nuestro planeta real?

Estoy interesada en jugar aquí con la paradoja entre los medios pictóricos tradicionales y la imagen digital, lo cual veo como analogía entre lo real y lo virtual. Estoy inclinada a trabajar con elementos opuestos; yuxtaponer el blanco y negro sobre el color, enfrentar la precisión del plano y la retícula (el píxel y la pantalla) contra la línea curva y la perspectiva no-Euclidiana.

Basada en los conceptos descritos por Paul Virilio y Pierre Lévy realicé en la sala principal de la galería Juan Salas en Bogotá, una instalación inmersiva con litografías sobre papel encolado y vinilo adhesivo cubriendo paredes piso

Hemispherical Immersion - Bogotá, Colombia -2013

opposite elements; juxtaposing black and white against a color, confronting a precise reticule of pixels to curved lines and to non Euclidean perspective.

y techo. Esta instalación se fusiona con el espacio expositivo donde se encuentran la piezas de la serie Panópticos y Panoramas. Una pieza de sonido desarrollada por Gilberto Castillo es parte de la instalación.

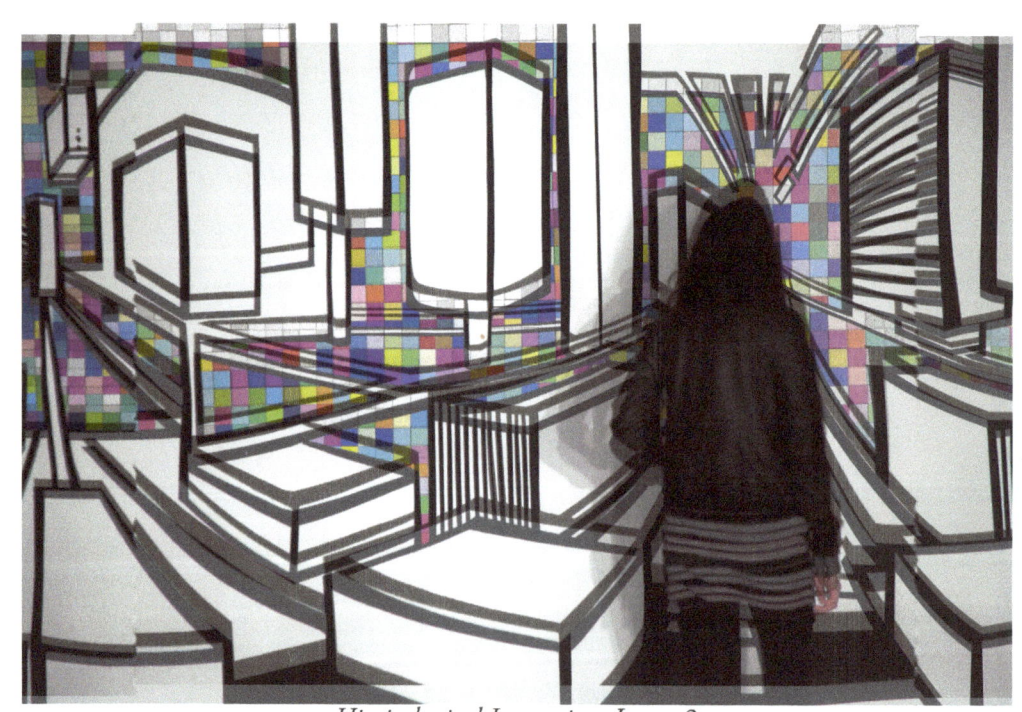

Himispherical Immersion: Image 2

Hemispherical Immersion - Bogotá, Colombia -2013

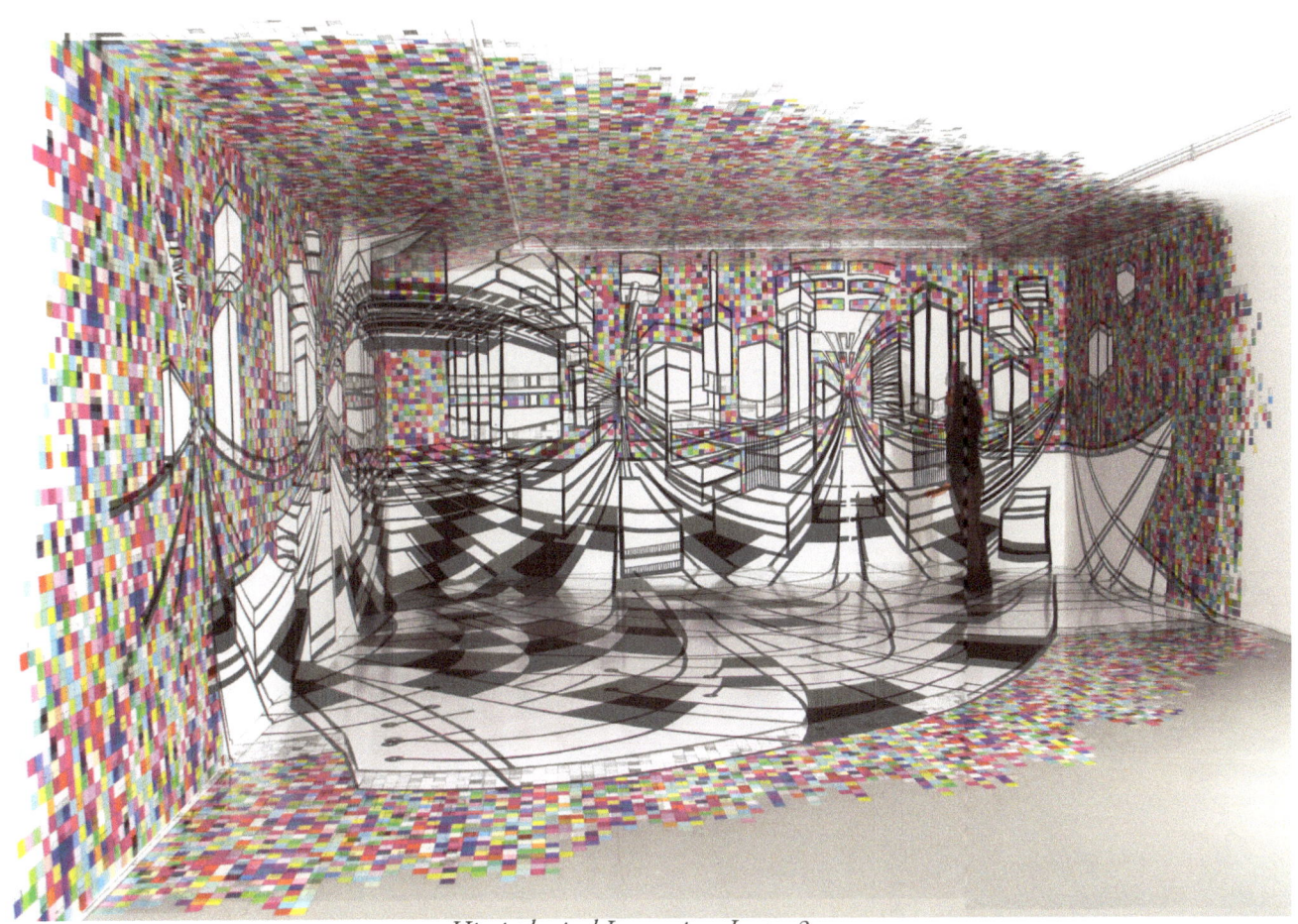

Himispherical Immersion: Image 3

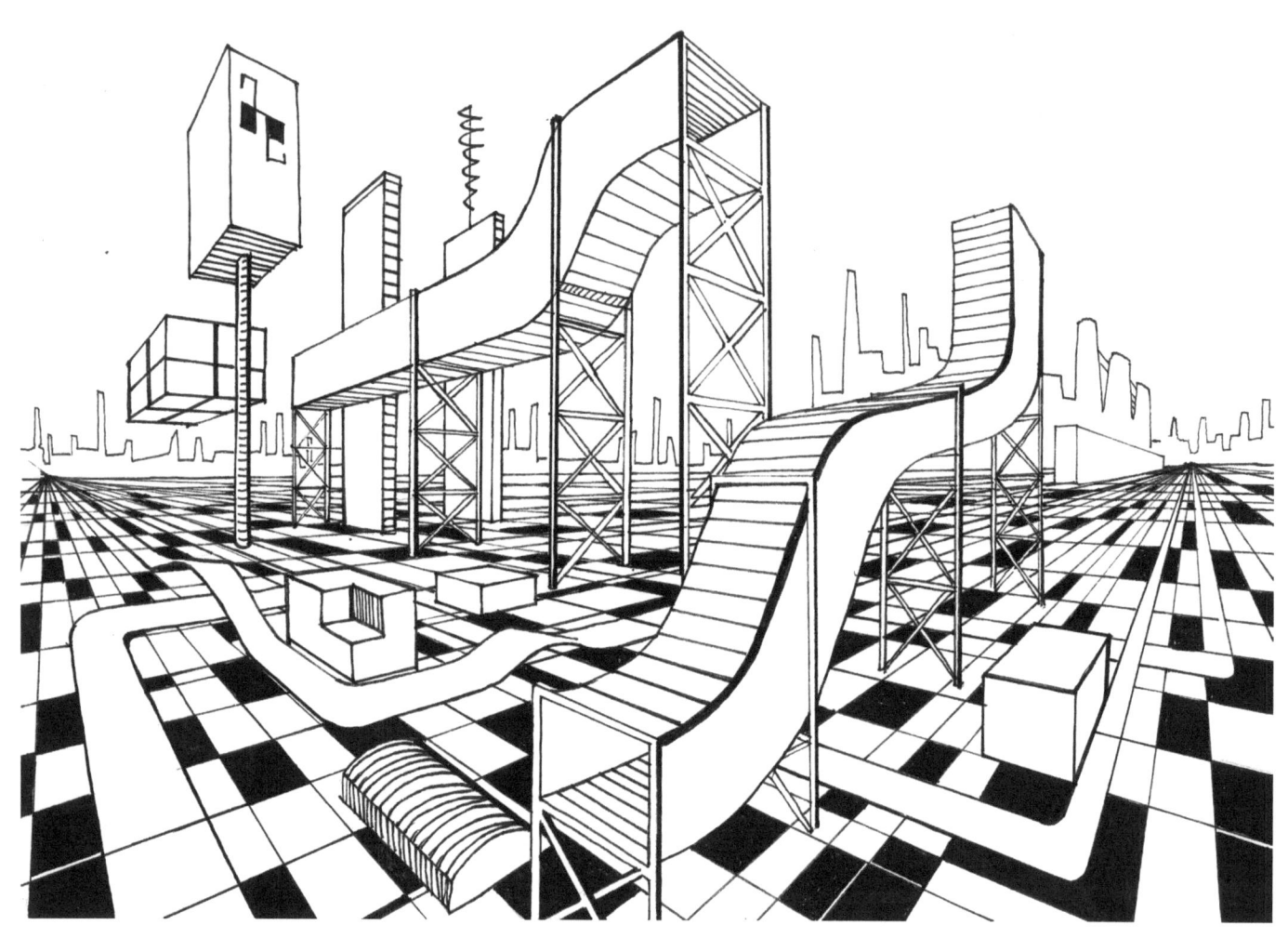

Untitled, 10" x 7" China Ink on Paper
Preliminary Sketch for ENTER THE WALL

Enter The Wall
Bogotá, Colombia 2012

Enter The Wall - 2012

ENTER THE WALL is a public space project that engages mural painting and video mapping manipulated live. Through this living piece I attempt to open new possibilities for mural work and video performance to be presented as one, exploring a multidisciplinary experience. Interested in exploring the relationship between time, medium, place and purpose I created an outdoor mural that in collaboration with other artists coupled 3 different mediums: painting, live video performance and sound design.

Inspired in Archigram and retro versions of the future, this black and white mural was video-mapped with live generative images, working as a screen that divided the real space against an artificially created depth. Like Alice through the looking glass, the piece invited people to cross the wall and enter a large scale, moving, imaginative world.

ENTERTHEWALL es un proyecto para el espacio público que integra la pintura mural con el video manipulado en vivo intentando abrir nuevas posibilidades para presentar estos dos medios como uno, explorando así posibilidades experimentales y experienciales a gran escala. Esta pieza explora la relación entre tiempo, medio, lugar y propósito a través de la yuxtaposición de medios de origen tradicional con medios tecnológicos integrando a artistas de tres disciplinas diferentes; dibujo y pintura, video y diseño sonoro.

Inspirado en Archigram y visiones retro del futuro, este mural en blanco y negro fue mapeado con imágenes generativas en vivo trabajando en conjunto como una pantalla que divide el espacio real sobre una profundidad creada artificialmente.

Enter The Wall - 2012

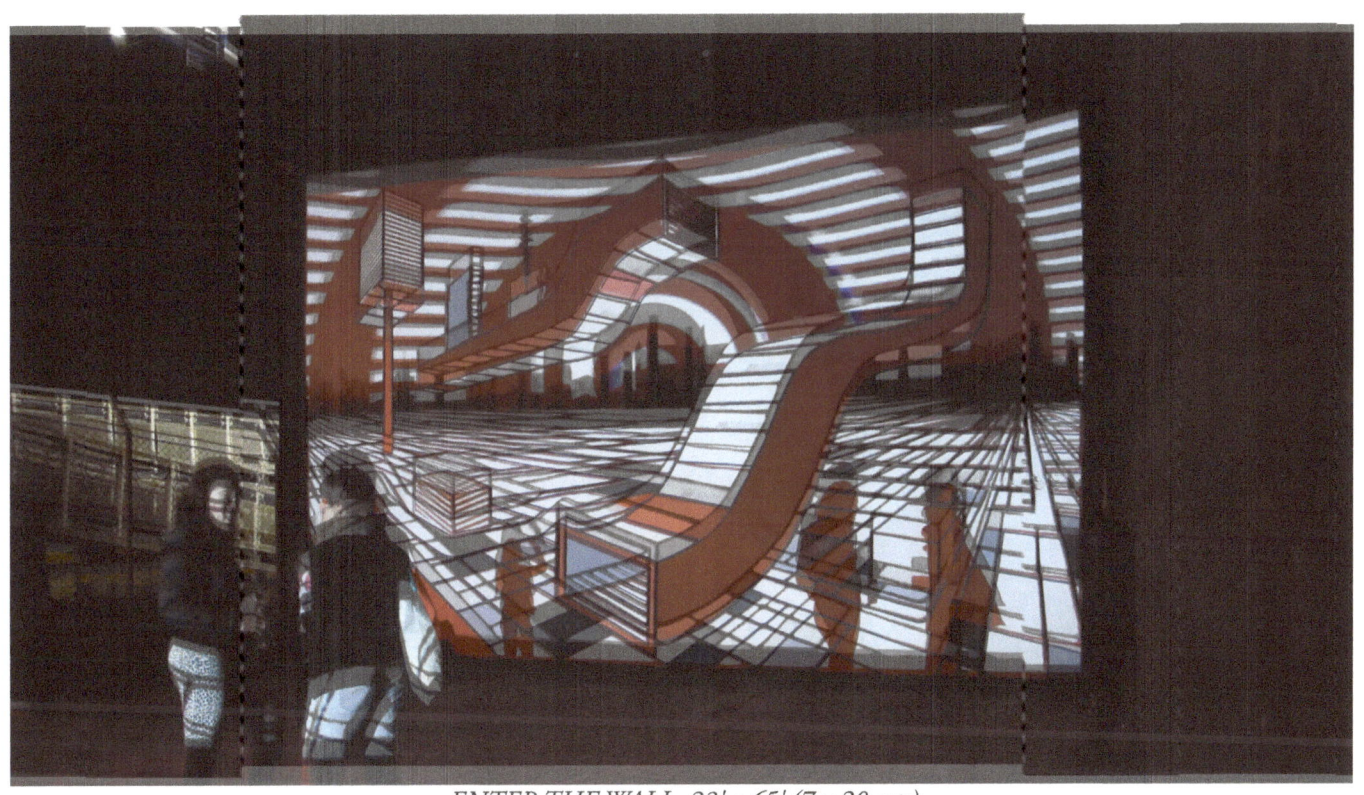

ENTER THE WALL, 23' x 65' (7 x 20 mts)
Acrylic Paint on Wall, Video Mapping Performance and Sound Design

Enter The Wall - 2012

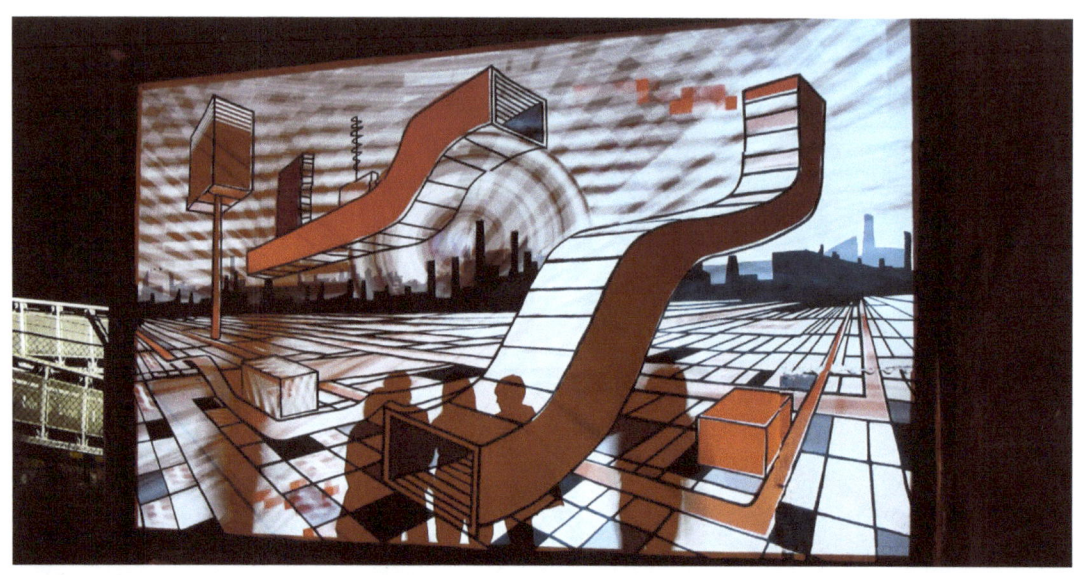

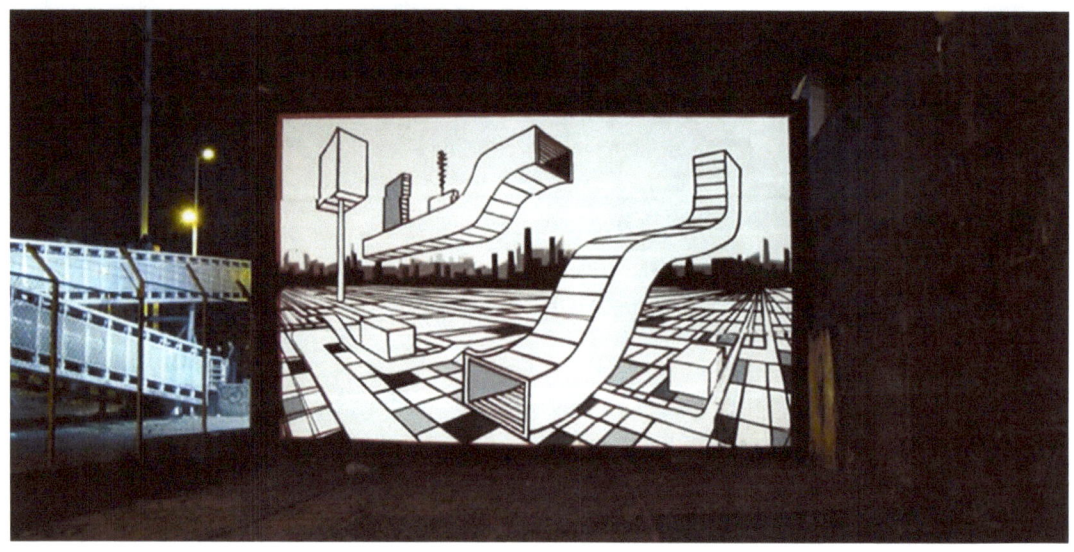

Enter The Wall - 2012

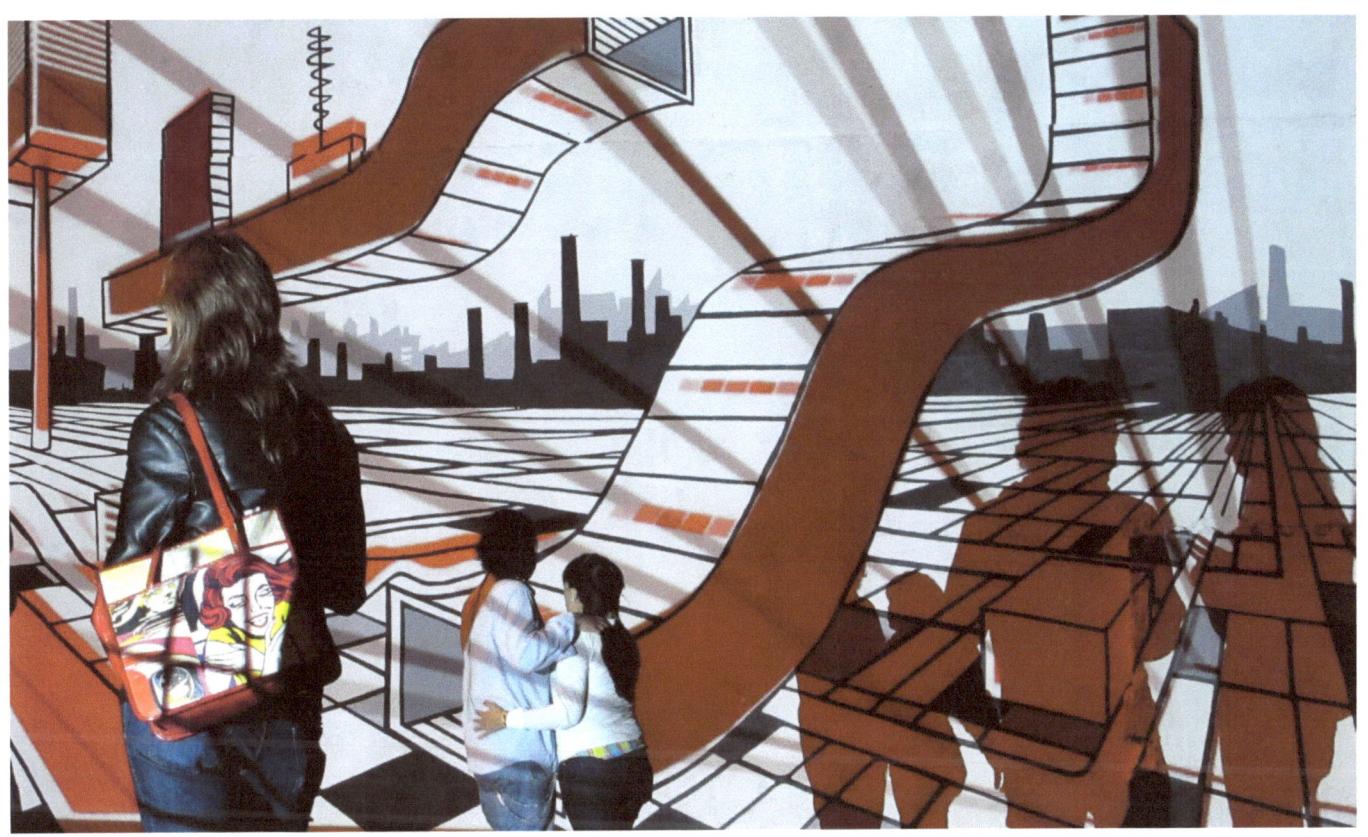

Mural painting and image composition: Jessica Angel.
Video mapping: Laura Ramirez. Music: Ivan Panqueva.

Pintura Mural y desarrollo de la imagen: Jessica Angel.
Video performance: Laura Ramírez. Música: Iván Panqueva.

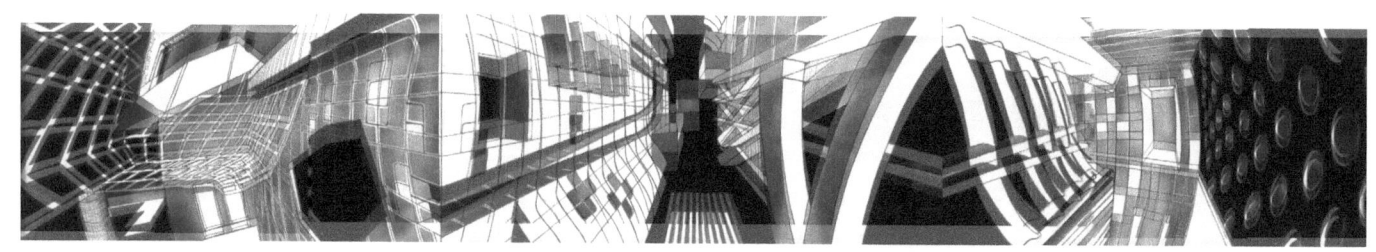

Cooper Union Building, 35" x 7" China Ink on Paper, Enamel on glass
Preliminary Sketch for The Self of the Building

The Self of the Building
The Cooper Union, NYC 2012

The Self of the Building - Cooper Union - NYC - 2012

"The Self of the Building" is an on-site mural installation inspired by the 41 Cooper Building. This futuristic structure is perhaps the most representative of the architectural utopian dreams in New York City. With this piece I show what I consider to be the "personality" of the building. The mural expresses how I interact with this massive monument. Archived material developed by architect Thom Mayne, my own photographs, sketches and the help of the wonderful Cooper Union interns and friends, were the necessary elements I needed to sustain this project until the very end.

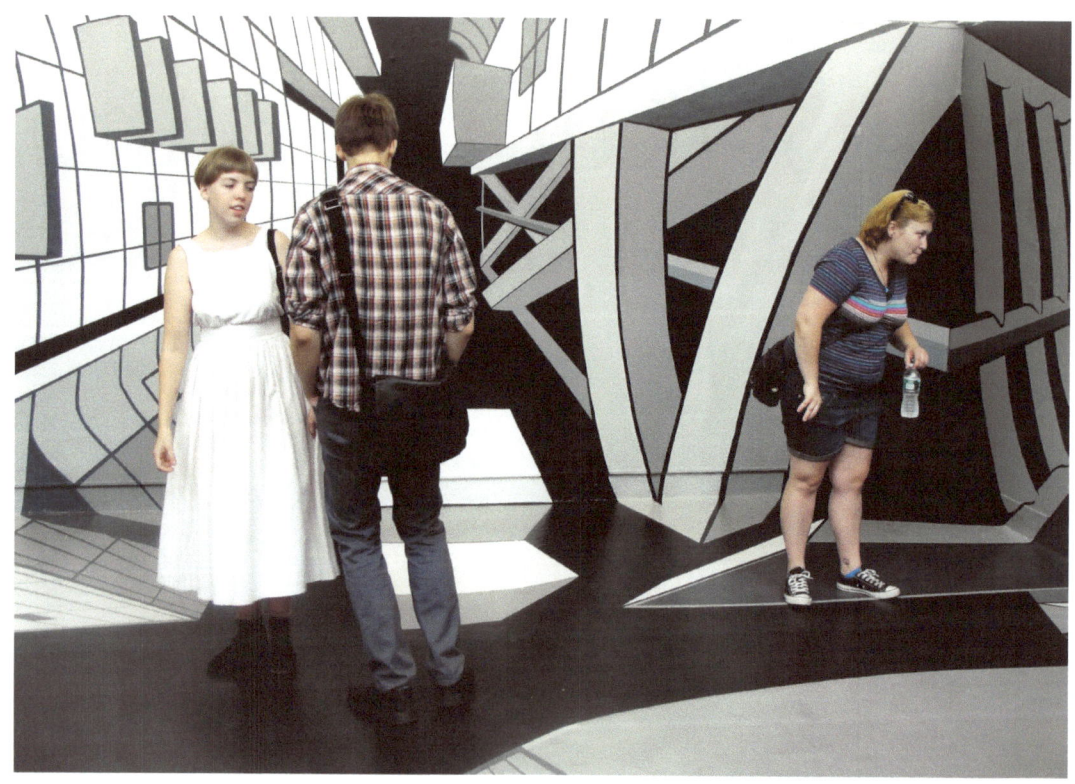

The Self of the Building. 16' x 18' x 8' (4.8 x 5.5 x 2.5 mts) Acrilyc Paint on walls and floor

The Self of the Building - Cooper Union - NYC - 2012

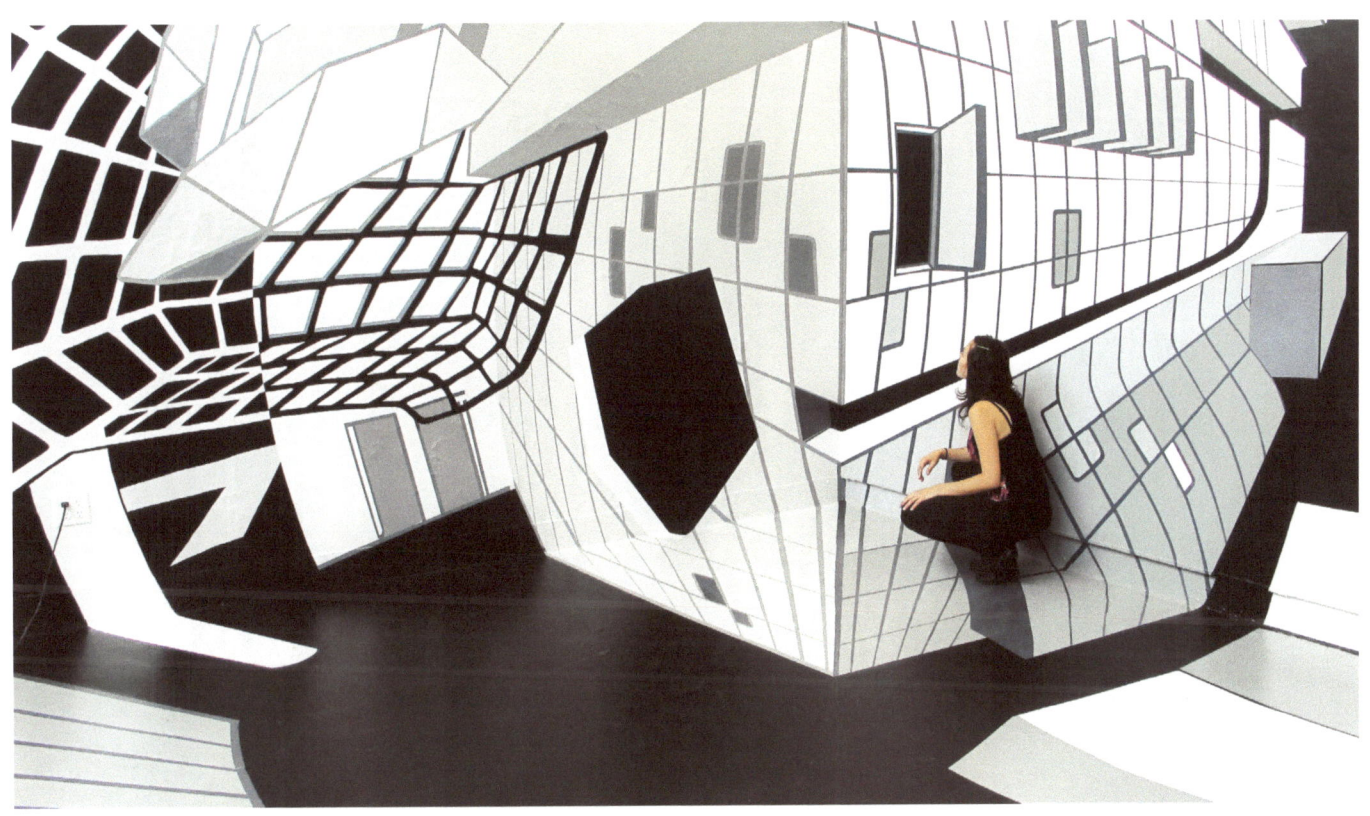

The Self of the Building. 16' x 18' x 8' (4.8 x 5.5 x 2.5 mts) Acrilyc Paint on walls and floor

Untitled, 10" x 7" China Ink on Paper
Preliminary Sketch for Building Code, 2010

Building Codes
Brooklyn, New York 2010

Building Codes - Downtown Brooklyn - NY - 2002

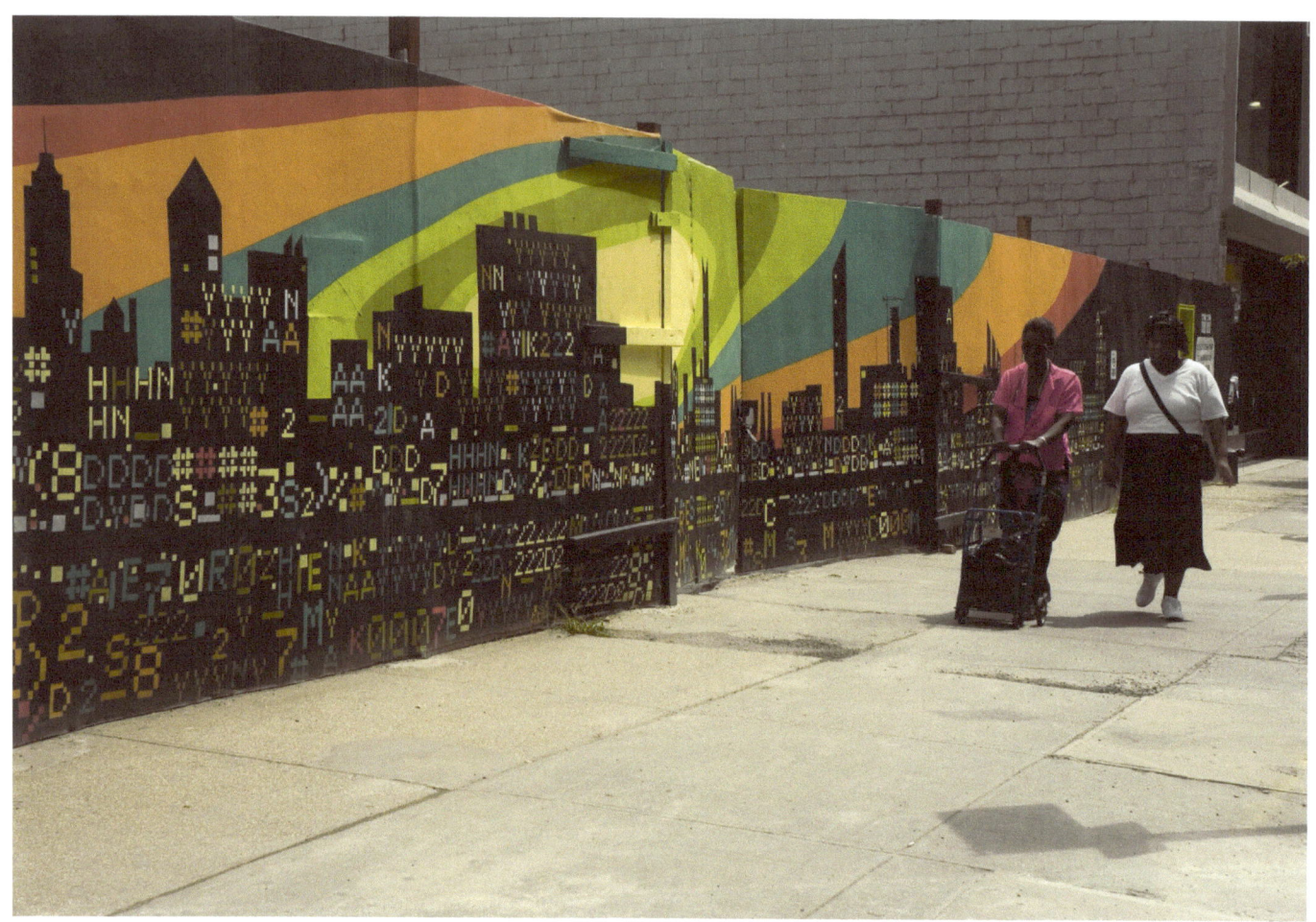

Building Codes - Acrylic on canvas installed on wood: w:60'x h:8'.

Building Codes - Downtown Brooklyn - NY - 2002

City Walls is a public art project commissioned by the MetroTech BID to enliven construction zones in the heart of Downtown Brooklyn. The BID solicited the arts consultancy services of BAC to curate the artists for City Walls and to facilitate the artwork installation. A construction site in Duffield St. between Willoughby St. and Fulton St. is home to the large-scale mural Building Codes. My work has been changing and mutating around the idea of massive media and information for the past years. I started doing cityscapes using magazine's paper as collage, I used newspapers as models for painting, legal and bureaucratic papers inspired my MFA thesis and the arrival of a new cyber-era that replaced all forms of information processes is the subject matter that leads my creations nowadays. Building Codes is hence, a cityscape made up of linguistic symbols and characters. The mural pretends to demonstrate how codes build our reality just as columns and walls give structure to the future building that is growing roots at this location.

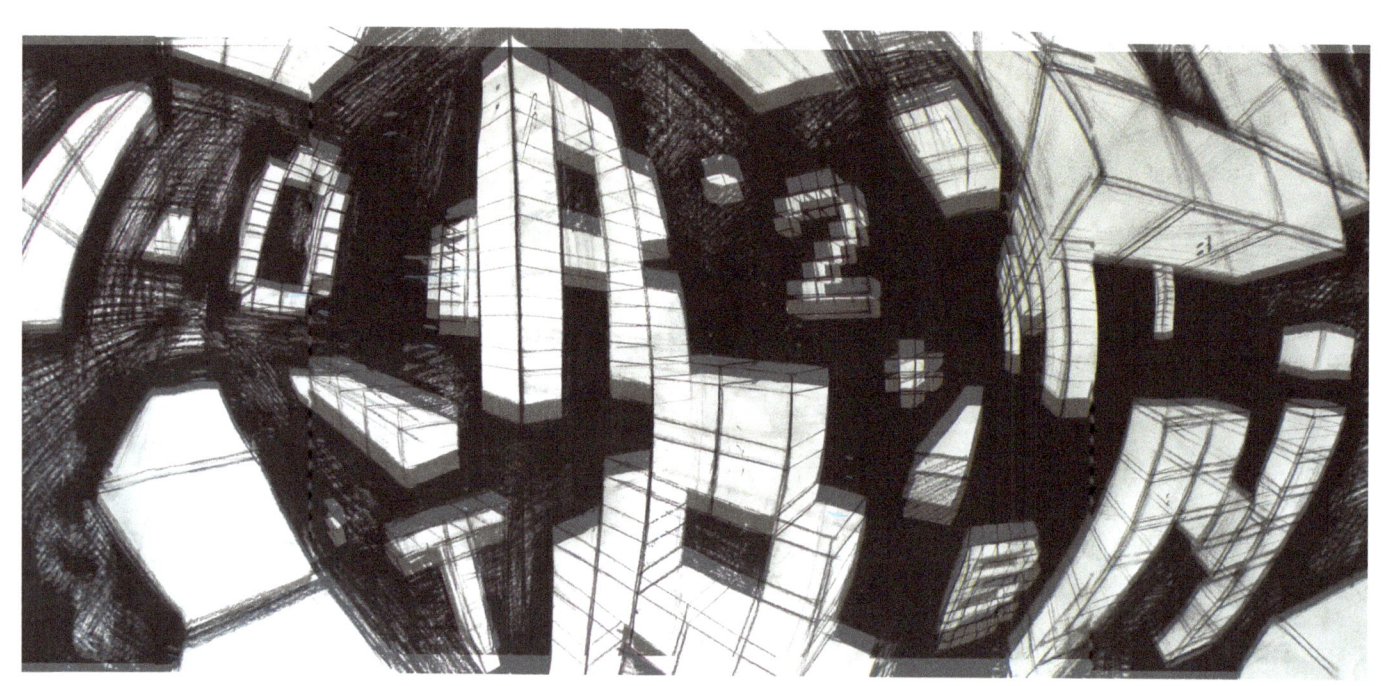

Floating Code. Preliminary Sketch for Info-Trek.
Charcoal on Paper. 30" x 15" 2009

Info-Trek

Brooklyn, New York 2009

Info-Trek - Brooklyn, New York - 2009

I had a dream not long ago where I was walking in this futuristic Tron like city, gigantic buildings and complexes rose above my head shining and spinning in psychedelic colors. The sound of computer machines seemed to be the language spoken by the people, it was a city where your five sense's even your sixth were invaded by cyber-information. I wake up and I realize how this hectic computer era is taking over our lives, awake or asleep. This whole global networking appeared now to me like a new domination system, just like what we read in "1984" or in "brave new world".

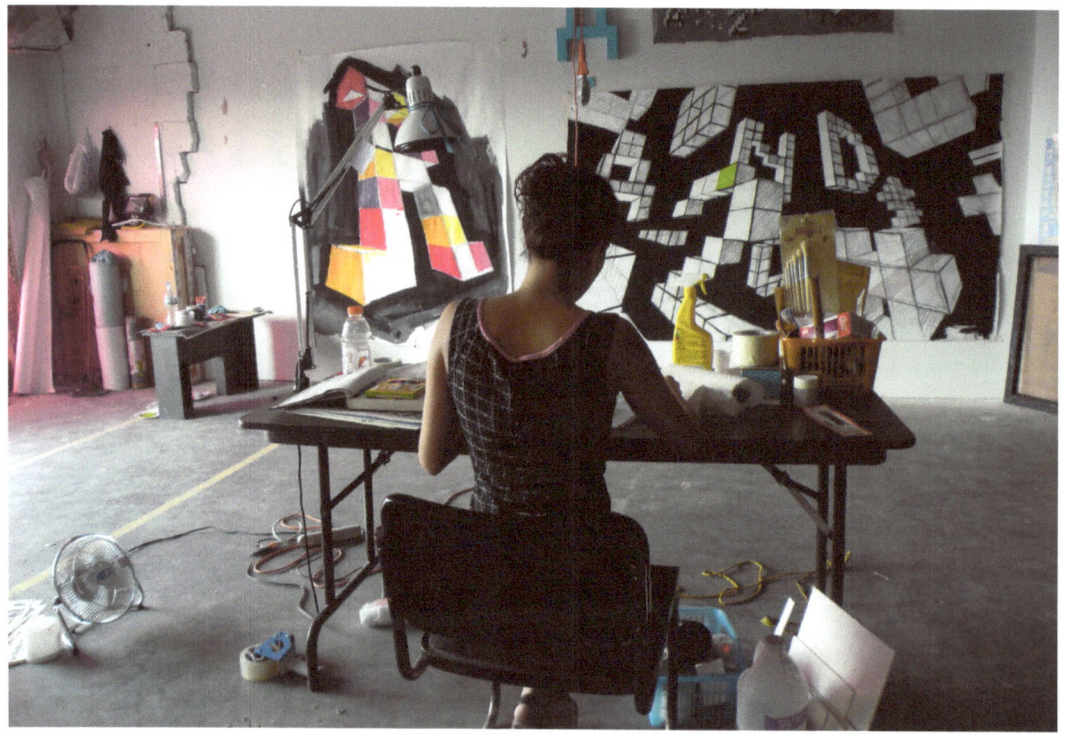

Jessica Angel workin in the One Brooklyn Bridge Park Building as a Resident Artist.
Brooklyn, NY. 2009

Info-Trek - Brooklyn, New York - 2009

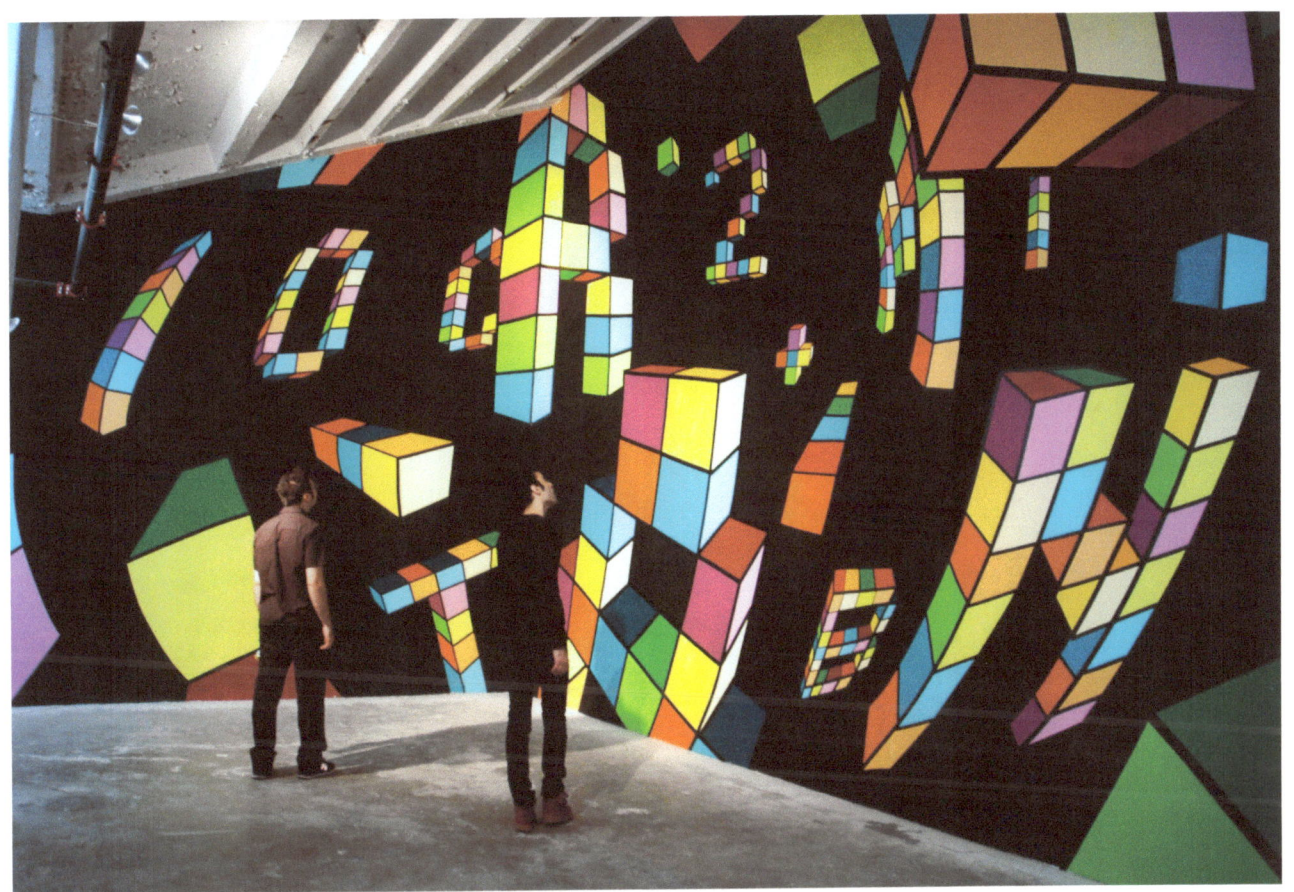

INFO-TREK. Acrylic paint and electrical tape on walls. 19' x 32' x 16'
Project developed during the artist in residency at BOFFO- NY

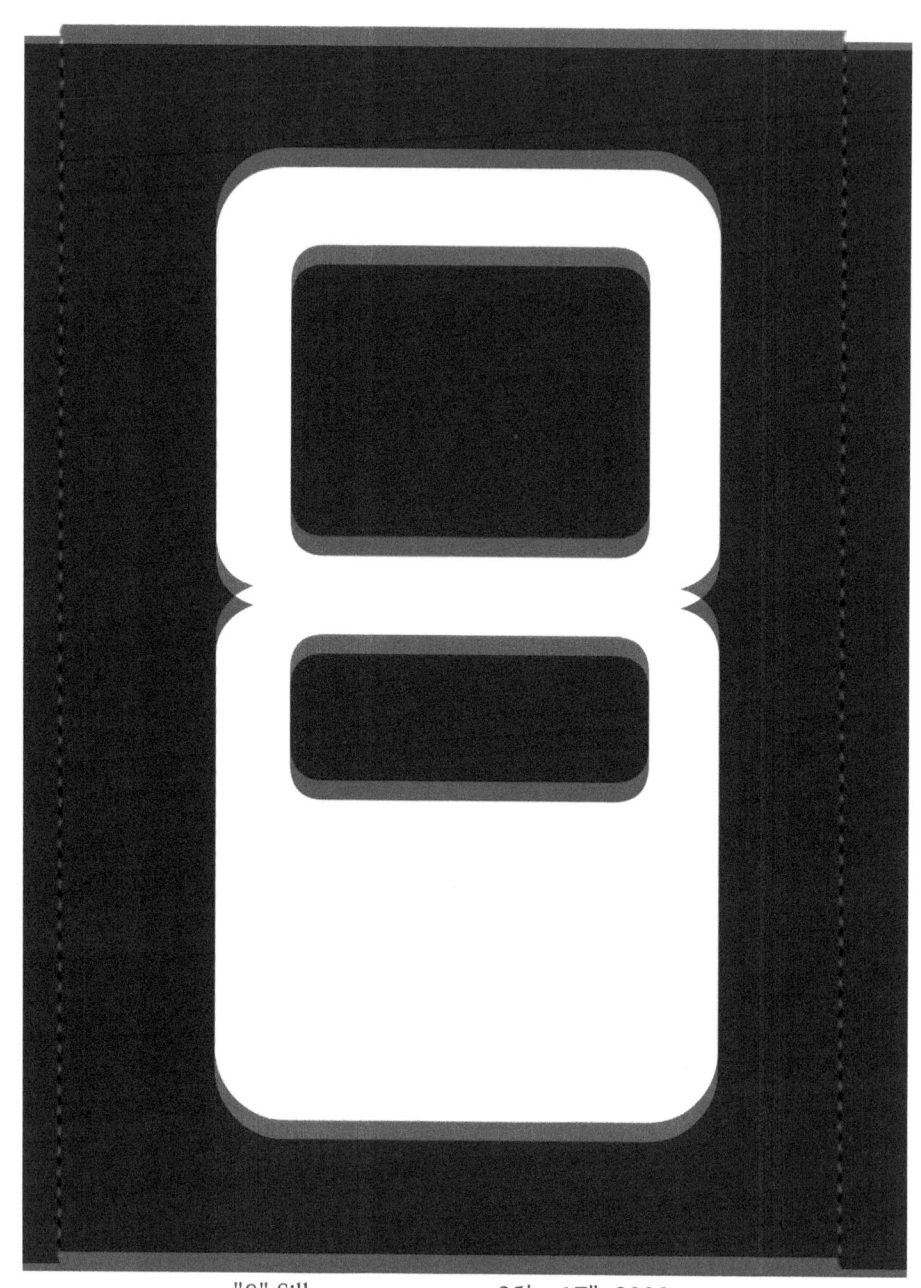

"8" Silkscreen on paper. 25' x 17". 2008
Paper used for the installation Inside the Computing Machine

Inside The Computing Machine
Bogotá, Colombia 2008

Inside The Computing Machine - Bogotá, Colombia - 2008

The installation Inside the Computing Machine (2008) allows us to enter a spaces in the shadows where thanks to a distant black light we can see characters and codes appear floating in all over the space. These pictorial prints affirm that this spatial immersion affects our senses. After we enter the space we feel attracted by the light, as if we were some kind of cyber-moths. From this angle of the space, the codes seem to radiate across the whole room. But they grow distant from the light, the fade into the deep black generating the sensation of unlimited depth. As we attempt to walk out the installation, we realize the space references have been erased… only the black curtain that covers the entrance allows us to put our feet back where reality is. The electronic sound piece that accompanies the installation increases the feeling of simulation.

La instalación Dentro de la máquina computadora (2008), nos permite adentrarnos en un espacio en penumbra donde gracias a luz negra, podemos ver algunos caracteres y códigos que parecen flotar en el espacio del piso al techo. Esas huellas "pictóricas" nos muestran que esa inmersión espacial afecta nuestros sentidos. Desde que entramos nos sentimos atraídos por la luz como una polilla cibernética. En ese ángulo del espacio, los códigos parecen irradiarse hacia toda la habitación. Pero a medida que avanzan se desdibujan en el negro profundo generando una sensación de profundidad ilimitada. Al disponernos al salir de la instalación, parecemos más bien adentrarnos en un espacio donde los referentes espaciales se han borrado… solamente la cortina negra que cubre la puerta, nos deja poner de nuevo los pies en la realidad. La música electrónica que acompaña la instalación afirma la sensación de simulación.

Inside The Computing Machine - Bogotá, Colombia - 2008

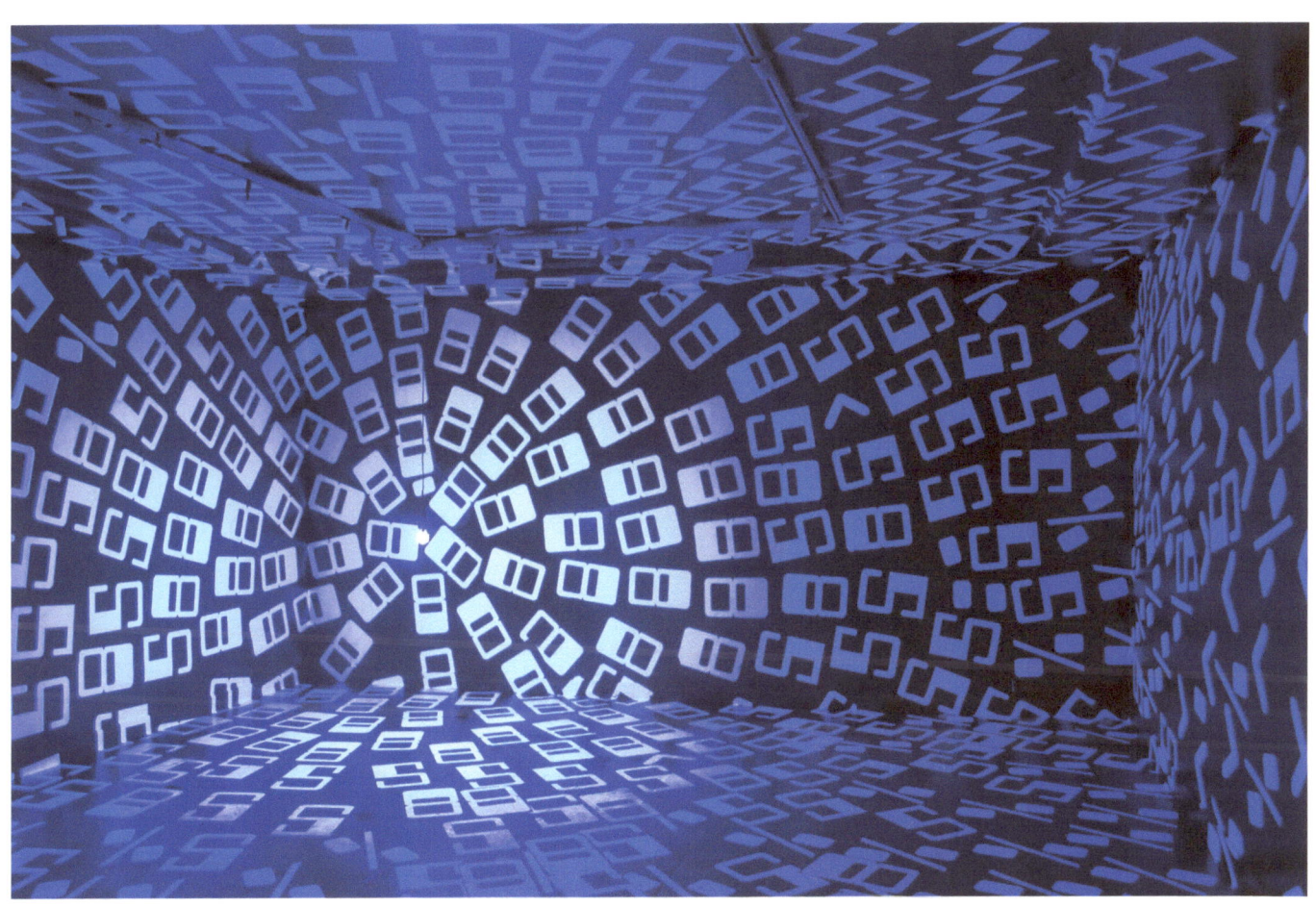

Inside the Computing Machine. Silkscreen prints on walls ceiling and floor. Sound design piece and black light
Size: 26' x 17' x 8'- Installation part of the exhibition ASCII Paintings and other attempts- 2008

Inside The Computing Machine - Bogotá, Colombia - 2008

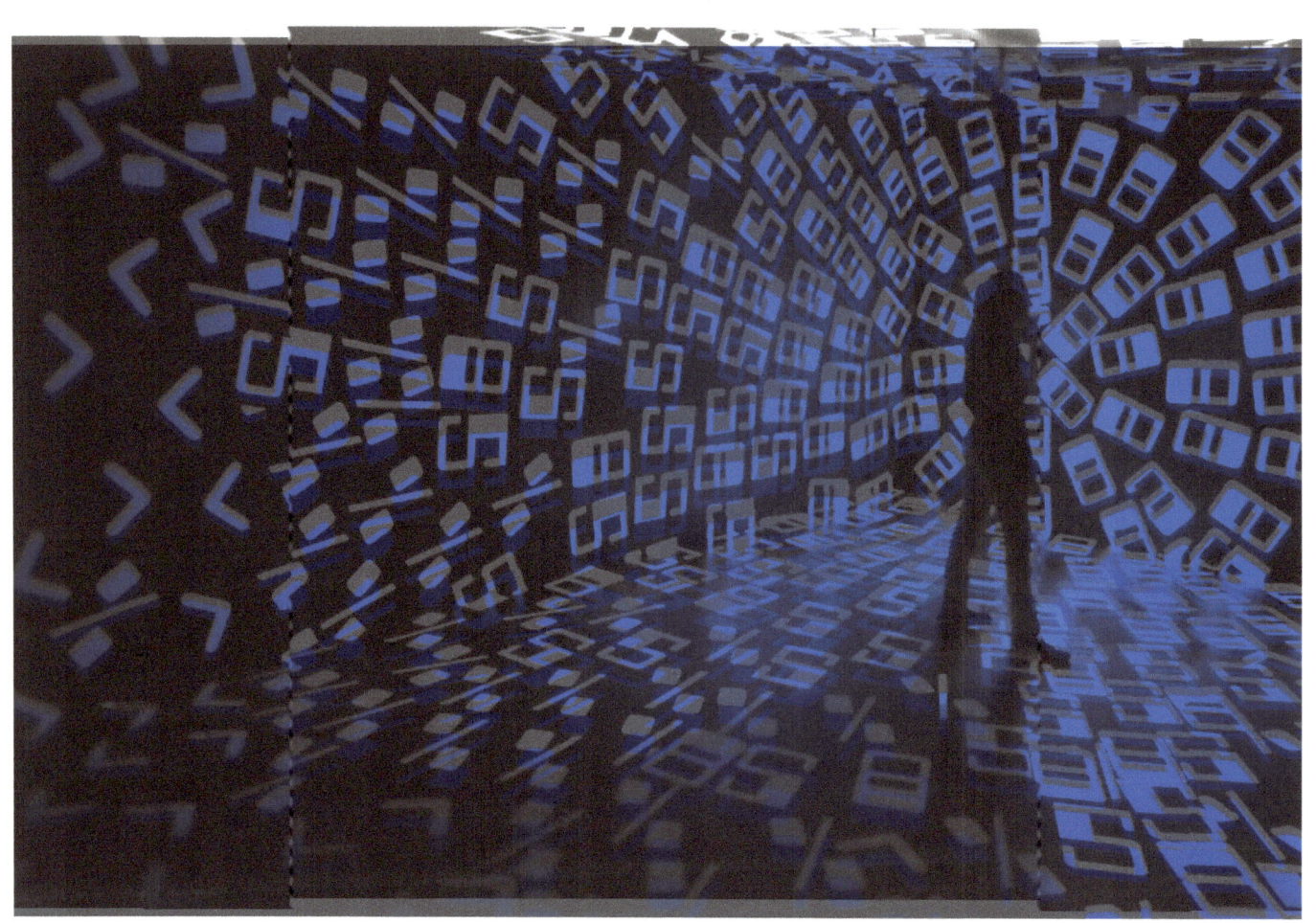

Inside the Computing Machine. Silkscreen prints on walls ceiling and floor. Sound design piece and black light
Size: 26' x 17' x 8' - Installation part of the exhibition ASCII Paintings and other attempts- 2008

Inside The Computing Machine - Bogotá, Colombia - 2008

There is no doubt this aesthetical experience alludes in an overwhelming way to the cybernetic immersion of digital media, where the computer transforms into this black box creator of sensations and new spaces. This works allows us to foresee a transit in painting to a different thing, similar to the experience that artist Juan Camilo Arango develops in his studio, filming his paintings and projecting them in the space. Is painting about to die? Or it's been dead for over two decades? Jessica Angel seems to affirm the opposite, insisting perhaps that there is a transformation of the pictorial practices, a transformation of the material form the immaterial that will still be contemporary painting.

Ricardo Arcos Palma
Fragment of "Contemporary Painting in Colombia," 2008

Sin duda, esta experiencia estética alude de forma contundente a la inmersión cibernética de los medios digitales, donde el computador se transforma en esa caja negra que crea sensaciones, nuevos espacios. Este trabajo nos hace prever un tránsito de la pintura a otra cosa como la experiencia que desarrolla el artista Juan Camilo Arango en su taller —que a propósito está por desaparecer por demolición–, filmando sus pinturas y proyectándolas en el espacio. La pintura está por morir o está muerta como se ha anunciado a los cuatro vientos desde hace ya más de dos décadas? Jessica Ángel parece afirmar lo contrario, insistiendo quizá que se trata más bien de una transformación de lo pictórico, de una transformación de lo material a lo inmaterial, pero seguirá siendo pintura contemporánea.

Ricardo Arcos Palma
Fragmento de "Pintura Contemporánea en Colombia / 2008

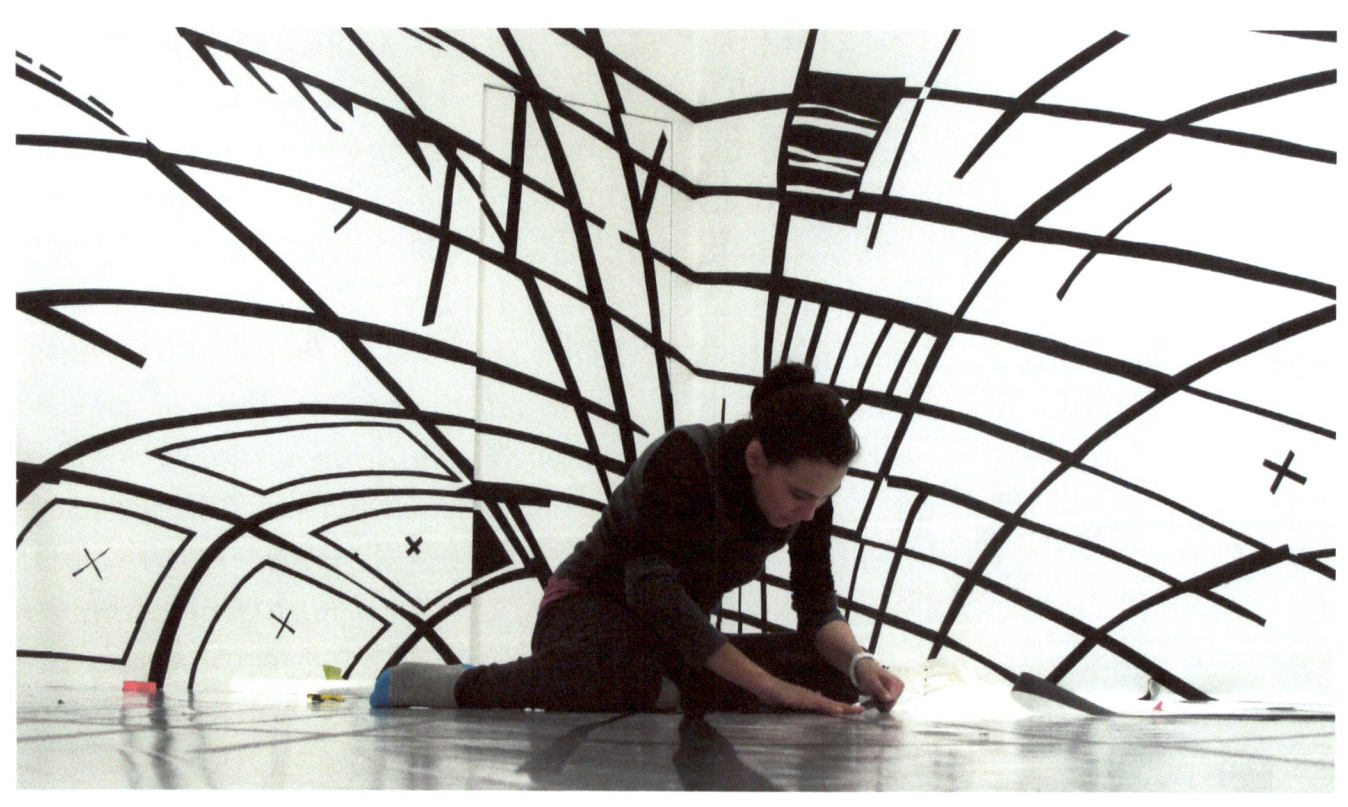

Jessica Angel working in the Installation As Above, So Below. New York - 2013

Jessica Angel

Panoptic, Panoramas and Hemespherical Immersions
By Conrado Uribe

Let's try to visualize a space and a time that takes place in the bridge that opens after questioning traditional and obsolete binary issues in regards to an upside and a downside, a north and a south, a body and a spirit, an object and a subject, two-dimensional and three-dimensional, real and virtual, etc. At the moment of dismantling the conventional dialectics supported by the opposition of contraries, and after embracing a complexity held in the proliferation of significant that may appear in the different positions, a possibility opens when contemplating the abyss, the absence of ground, the loss of a rigid surface. However, this is not the attraction towards the abyss by the romantic type of thought. There aren't now neither summits nor masts from where to scan a panorama with an identifiable

Intentemos visualizar un espacio y un tiempo ubicados justo en la brecha que se abre tras cuestionar binarismos tradicionales y obsoletos con respecto a un arriba y un abajo, norte y sur, cuerpo y espíritu, objeto y sujeto, bidimensional y tridimensional, realidad y virtualidad, etc. Al desmantelar la dialéctica convencional soportada en la oposición de contrarios, y abrazar una complejidad soportada en la proliferación de significantes que pueden aparecer entre las diferentes posiciones, se abre la posibilidad de contemplar el abismo, la ausencia de suelo, la pérdida de un soporte rígido. Pero no es esta la atracción por el abismo del pensamiento romántico. Ahora no quedan cumbres ni mástiles desde los cuales otear un panorama que tiene un horizonte identificable (así fuera tan inestable como el océano o un mar de nubes); un plano de llegada en caso de

horizon (even if it was as unstable as the ocean or a sea of clouds); a field of arrival in case of a fall; an infinite void. How does this situation leave us? Suspended in a constant fall, just like Hito Steyerl proposes; floating in an apparent stranded situation while everything around us, including ourselves keeps falling. Considering this condition of absence of bases, nothing seems to advance, not even in space, not even in time. And we forget as a consequence, that there was a time when this apriori way of the internal sensibility did (time according to Kant); determining the structure of history and the substitute idea of progress. The resultant agitation enables the confusion between categories that would distinguish a subject from the things that surrounded it; to what came before an what would come after; to what was above from what was below; the private field to the public sphere; kitsch from good taste; tangible from its virtual counterpart.

arrojo, un vacío finito. fuera tan inestable como el océano o un mar de nubes); un plano de llegada en caso de arrojo, un vacío finito. ¿Cómo nos deja esta situación? Suspendidos en permanente caída libre como lo propone Hito Steyerl, flotando en una aparente situación de estancamiento mientras todo lo que nos rodea, incluyéndonos, sigue cayendo. Ante esa condición de ausencia de bases nada parece avanzar, ni siquiera el tiempo o el espacio. Y olvidamos en consecuencia que hubo una época en la que esa forma a priori de la sensibilidad interna —el tiempo según Kant= lo hacía, determinando la estructuración de la historia y la idea de progreso sucedánea. La agitación resultante propicia la confusión entre categorías que distinguían a un sujeto de las cosas que le rodeaban; a lo que venía antes de lo que iba después; a lo que estaba encima de lo que estaba debajo; el campo de lo privado de la esfera pública; el kitsch del buen gusto; a lo tangible de su contraparte virtual.

49

And how does this echo in the visual field? From over a century, the western paradigm determined by renaissance perspective comes from a dismantling and deconstructive progressive process. The horizon, in its equilibrium and its apparent linearity, has been questioned by cinema and its montage possibilities; by modern painting and by collage;. Also by quantum physics and the theory of relativity; by transportation media and by communication technology. These series of events transform and increase the perspectives, opening the space to other visual forms.

Does this contingency permit the experience of freedom? Many of the same gains gained from contemporaneity have favored the upraise of new totalitarian states, where the place of control and vigilance is not located in buildings or institutions, but through the same infrastructure that promised the speed that bordered immediacy; the equality

¿Y cómo repercute esto en el campo de la visualidad? Desde hace más de un siglo el paradigma occidental determinado por la perspectiva renacentista viene en un progresivo proceso de deconstrucción y desmantelamiento. El horizonte, los horizontes, en su equilibrio y linealidad aparentes, han sido cuestionados por el cine y su posibilidad de montaje; por la pintura moderna y el collage; por la física cuántica y la teoría de la relatividad; por los medios de transporte; por las tecnologías de la comunicación. Esta serie de remezones transforman y aumentan las perspectivas, abriendo campo necesariamente a otras formas de lo visual.

¿Posibilita ésta contingencia la experiencia de la libertad? Han sido muchas de las mismas ganancias de la contemporaneidad las que han favorecido el surgimiento de nuevos estados de totalitarismo, en los que la vigilancia y el control no tienen lugar en edificios o instituciones, sino a través de

of conditions y the rupture- Finally!_- of the monolithic identities in fields like gender and nationality; the demographic access to information, its collective construction and the questioning to hegemonic centers that had generated and spread.

Can we keep talking about virtual reality as the binary opposite, dialectic, metaphysical, of a more ordinary, corporeal, daily reality? How virtual are realities that have been denominated this way, when who have global control over info-economic fluxes can turn upside down all the social and political gains of a world that believed in the ideas of the modern project? After seeing the breaking of society's well being, and the fall of the triumph of middle classes, how is it possible to keep the gained freedom? Is it possible to depict the horizon of these new augmented realities making use meanwhile of materials that are not

la propia infraestructura que prometió la velocidad que lindaba con la inmediatez; la igualdad de condiciones y la fractura —¡por fin! – de las identidades monolíticas en campos como el género y la nacionalidad; el acceso democrático a la información, su construcción colectiva y el cuestionamiento a los centros hegemónicos que la habían generado y difundido.

¿Podemos seguir hablando de realidad virtual como el opuesto binario, dialéctico, metafísico de una realidad más ordinaria, corpórea y cotidiana? ¿Qué tan virtuales son las realidades así denominadas, cuando quienes tienen el control global de los flujos informático-económicos pueden poner patas arriba todas las ganancias sociales y políticas de un mundo que creyó en los ideales del proyecto moderno? Tras ver el modo en que la sociedad del bienestar y el triunfo de las clases medias se resquebraja y se cae a pedazos, ¿cómo es posible conservar las libertades ganadas? ¿Es posible

Here we find the accuracy of Jessica Angel, in the risk of assuming this last challenge from such traditional techniques as painting and serigraphy; without fear to address pixels through paint (exercise she started a few years from now); to approaching three dimensions as of two-dimensional procedures; or to avail in her proposals the instability, the aperture, the deterritorialization. Are we floating or falling in her installations? Are we above or are we below? Are we another thing among those suspended realities? The vertigo generated in her installations is emancipating; the absence of ground and horizon simply through us to the changing formations of contemporary realities.

Aquí está el acierto de Jessica Ángel, en el riesgo de asumir este último reto desde técnicas tan tradicionales como la pintura y la serigrafía; sin temor a hablar de píxeles a través de pigmentos (tarea que ya emprendió desde hace varios años); a atacar las tres dimensiones a partir de procedimientos bidimensionales; o a acoger en su propuesta la inestabilidad, la apertura, la desterritorialización. ¿Flotamos o caemos en su instalación? ¿Estamos arriba o abajo? ¿Somos una cosa más dentro de aquellas realidades suspendidas? El vértigo que generan sus instalaciones es liberador; la ausencia de suelo y horizontes solo nos arroja a la formación cambiante de las realidades actuales.

About Jessica Angel

Jessica Angel is a visual artist living and working between Bogota and New York. Her recent and upcoming projects aim to foster cross-disciplinary initiatives. She was invited to represent Colombia as an artist in residence at the 2014 Vancouver Biennale, where she will develop a project enabling forms of collaboration among sciences, philosophy, music, art and new media. In 2013 she organized Pintura Abierta, a collaborative project that prompted the circulation of ideas about painting. In an attempt to consider this language through its practice, the creation and reflection laboratory gathered different proposals by Colombian painters by means of on-site paintings. The project took place in the Parqueadero space of the Museo del Banco de la República.

While living in New York City Jessica has been awarded the Teaching-Artist Residency at the Cooper Union, the BRIC Media Arts Fellowship (2012), City Walls with the Brooklyn Arts Council (2010) and the BOFFO Artist in Residence (2009). She has exhibited solo at Juan Salas Gallery (2012), The Museum of Modern Art of Bucaramanga (2008), at the Salamanca University Cultural Center in Bogotá (2008), at The Project Room of Los Andes University in Bogota and at Casas Riegner Gallery (2006 and 2009). Her work has been exhibited both locally and abroad in cities like Bogota, New York, Miami, Washington, Rosario, La Paz and Mexico. In 2007 she received an honorable mention at the 4th International Biennial SIART, Bolivia and at the 1st Drawing Biennial of the Americas, Mexico (2006).

wwww.jessicaangelarts.com

SOLO EXHIBITIONS
2013 Panoptics and Panoramas. Juan Salas Gallery. Bogota, Colombia
2009 Dirty Worthless Money. Casas Riegner Gallery, Bogota Colombia
2008 Virtual Windows. Museum of Modern Art, Bucaramanga, Colombia
2008 The Architecture of Hypertext. Universidad de los Andes. Project Space. Bogota
2007 ASCII Paintings and Other Attempts. Salamanca University. Bogota.
2006 The Papers of the Law. Casas Riegner Gallery, Bogota, Colombia

SITE-SPECIFIC PROJECTS
2013 Hemispherical Immersions. Juan Salas Gallery. Bogota, Colombia
2012 Enter the Wall. Public Art Istallation. Bogotá, Colombia
2012 The Self of the Building. The Cooper Union New York, NY
2010 Building Codes. Brooklyn Arts Council, NY
2009 Info-Trek. One Brooklyn bridge Park Building. Brooklyn, NY
2007 Urbania. Public Art Intervention. IV Biennial SIART. La Paz, Bolivia

DISCTINTIONS AND AWARDS
2013 "El Parqueadero" Bank of the Republic of Colombia and FGGA
2012 BRIC Media Arts fellowship
2012 Teaching Artist-Summer Residency, Cooper Union, New York, NY
2010 City Walls -Brooklyn Arts Council. New York
2009 BOFFO-Artist in Residence. Brooklyn, NY
2007 Honorable Mention. V International Arte Biennial SIART La Paz. Bolivia
2006 Honorable Mention. I Drawing Biennial of the Americas. Mexico
2006 Meritor Thesis. Universidad Nacional de Colombia. Bogotá

SELECTED GROUP EXHIBITIONS
2013
Converging Cultures. Martin Rutherford Galleries. VA
Form and Substance - Gowanus Ballroom. Brooklyn, NY
Blank Canvas Benefit. Visual Arts Center of New Jersey
2012
Nuevos Espacios Pictoricos, Bucaramanga, Colombia
SAW. Public art project Bay Ridge, Brooklyn
2011
Slideluck Potshow -Bushwick Emerging Artists. Ward 3, Brooklyn, NY
Bushwick Open Studios. Troutman Studios Building. # 256
Up Close and Personal. Vandalog and M.A.N.Y. New York

SELECTED GROUP EXHIBITIONS

2010
SMALL WORKS, In Rivers Gallery, Greenpoint , NY
200 Years of Art in Colombia. Museum of Modern Art. Bogota, Colombia.
City Walls. Large-scale mural in Duffield and Fulton. Brooklyn Arts Council.
Bushwick Open Studios. Troutman Studios Building. # 256
iEmotions. Abaca. Apexart. New York, NY
Design on Dime, Housing Works Benefit. Metropolitan Pavilion. NY
G40. The Summit. Art Whino Gallery, Washington D.C.

2009
Double Scoop Cityscape. Long View Gallery, Washington DC.
OBJECTIVE AFFECTION, BOFFO, Large Scale Mural at One Brooklyn Bridge Park.
Yo Veo. International Video festival, The Suffolk Space. New York, NY
Urban Development. Curated by Joe Fig. LES Printshop. New York, NY

2008
Four Latin American Painters, Praxis International Gallery, Miami, USA
Characters. Camara de Comercio de Bogota. Sede Salitre. Colombia
ArtBodegon. Independent Artists Space, El Bodegón, Bogotá
Cuestión de Coraz?n. El Museo Gallery, Bogotá

2007
ARTBO 2007. Bogota International Art Fair. Artecámara Pavillion. Corferias,
Arte Joven, Mundo Gallery, Bogotá
Por Pintar Cu4rto Nivel Foundation. Bogotá, Colombia
Columnas UN, From the colective project; Art, City, University and Culture.
Solidarte, El Museo Gallery, Bogotá

2006
International Drawing Biennial of the Americas. La Galería de la Ciudad, México
ARTBO 2006, Bogota International Art Fair, Casas Riegner Gallery booth
CINCO ARTISTAS / FIVE ARTISTS Casas Riegner Gallery. Bogotá

2005
104 Art Suites Site specific project in the lobby space. Bogotá
XII Latinamerican Video Festival 2005, Electronic arts show. Experimenta Colombia. Rosario, Argentina

2004
Young Colombian Artists Foundation. Bogotá
XXXI Cano Salon Art Museum, National University of Colombia.
Citiexposiciones 2004 Young Colombian Artists Foundation. Bogotá

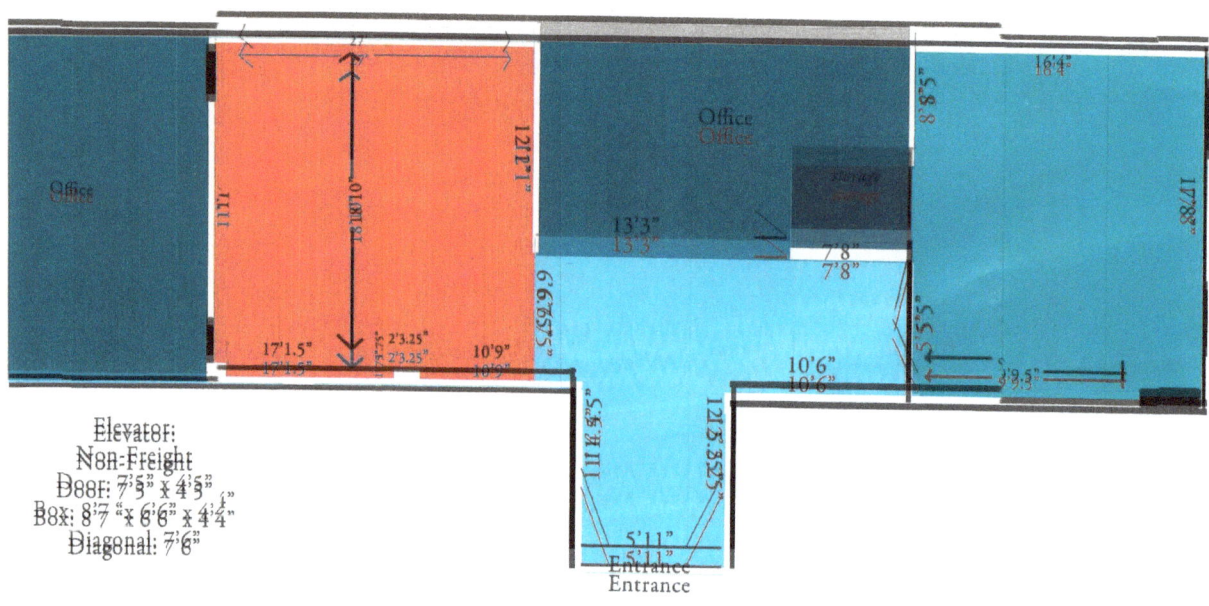

All images are courtesy of the artist unless otherwise noted.

Special Thanks

Interns
Candace Fong - Katrina Kajkut - Clair Kleinman - Teri Minogue

The AC Institute
Holly Crawford - Eliana Blechman - Eddy Villatoro - Nicole Bebout
James Dillenbeck

For their Support and Assistance
Andres Angel - Juan Camilo Arango - Michael Friedman - Kika Lievano
Monica Vasquez

Project Collaborators
Jaclyn Avidon - Gilberto Castillo - Live Footage - Soler - Nelson Ramon

www.ingramcontent.com/pod-product-compliance
Lightning Source LLC
Chambersburg PA
CBHW051918210526
45473CB00006B/2058